Cracking Open the Author's Craft

Teaching the Art of Writing

Lester L. Laminack

■SCHOLASTIC

Cover design by Adana Jimenez
Cover illustration by Jorge J. Namerow
Cover photograph © Geoff Spear/Veer
Interior design by Maria Lilja
Acquiring Editor: Lois Bridges
Production Editor: Raymond Coutu
Copy Editor: Ellen Tarlin
Video production, design, and development by Michael Gibbons and John Gayle

Scholastic is not responsible for the content of third-party websites and does not endorse any site
or imply that the information on the site is error-free, correct, accurate, or reliable.

ISBN-13: 978-1-338-13452-0
ISBN-10: 1-338-13452-3

Scholastic is constantly working to lessen the environmental impact of our manufacturing processes.
To view our industry-leading paper procurement policy, visit www.scholastic.com/paperpolicy.

1 2 3 4 5 6 7 8 9 10   40   25 24 23 22 21 20 19 18 17 16

 Text pages printed on 10% PCW recycled paper.

*To Zachary Seth Laminack, my joy, my pride. No matter
what I accomplish in this life, you will remain my single
most significant contribution to this universe. I am proud
of the man you have become. You are a talented writer with
a bright future. Remember—vision, tenacity, kindness.
I am honored to be your Papa.*

*And in memory of
my mom, Mary Jo Thompson Laminack,
and
my mammaw, Zella Mozelle Watson Thompson*

Contents

Contents of the Online Resource Bank

Explore the Author's Craft With Lester L. Laminack

scholastic.com/authorcraft

Acknowledgments

Much like a rock formation in the desert is shaped by constant wind, occasional rain, dust storms and blowing sands, the scorching heat of day and the quick cooling of night, this project has been shaped over time by many minds. I owe a debt of gratitude to writers who have influenced my notions of style and voice and craft. I owe a debt of gratitude to teachers of writing who have influenced my notions of how best to teach others to write and how best to lead teachers who teach young writers. I owe a debt of gratitude to editors who asked the right questions at the right time to push my insights and writing to the next plateau. So let me attempt to pay that debt.

As a writer of children's picture books, I am influenced by the many books I read. All writers work under the influence of their reading life. But there are five writers whose work I return to over and over. I find new things to marvel at each time I read and reread their work. So, to these five writers, I am grateful for the talents you share:

- Mem Fox, dear friend, I marvel at your command of just-right words and control of rhythm. You are a master of big messages in few words. And more importantly, your heart is so kind.

- Patricia MacLachlan, though I have met you only twice, I swim in the soft currents of your language and dance to the music of your writing.

- Tony Johnston, though we have met only briefly, I am amazed by the sheer volume and range of your work. I delight in the playfulness of Anna and Amber and weep at the pain of The Harmonica.

- Jacqueline Woodson, though we have only been introduced to one another in a convention hall booth, I so admire your willingness to take on the tough issues in the lives of children.

You do it with kindness and truth. You do it with care and courage. You do it with grace and elegance. Thank you.

- Cynthia Rylant, though I have never met you and may never meet you face to face, I feel as though I know you. I get lost in the places you create; I float on the beauty of your words.

As a teacher of writers and as a teacher of the teachers of writers, I am influenced by the thinking, teaching, and writing of the many teachers I meet and work alongside. I am influenced as I listen to them speak at conferences and institutes, and when I read their thoughts and insights in articles and professional books. But there are a few to whom I owe specific thanks:

- Katie Ray (aka Katie Wood Ray), dearest friend, longtime colleague, cowriter, thinking partner. I learn and stretch each time I am in your company, whether you are speaking to thousands or talking over lunch. I cherish our friendship and honor your insightful mind

- Ralph Fletcher, I first met you in the pages of *What a Writer Needs*. I have been learning from you ever since. This book remains the most influential book on my life as a writer. Later I came to know you and your writing for children. I still relish the music of *Twilight Comes Twice* each time I read it aloud. I am proud to call you friend.

- Lucy Calkins, I first knew you through *Lessons from a Child* and then through *The Art of Teaching Writing*. I recognized your insightful mind and knew I could learn from you. More recently I have come to know you through my participation and teaching in the summer reading and writing institutes at Teachers College. I have had the opportunity to think with you, and I continue to grow both personally and professionally as a result.

Each of you has had a significant impact on my thinking. I have greater depth of understanding about writing and the teaching of writing because of the work you have done and your willingness to share your thinking. My thanks to you.

As a professional writer, I have had the opportunity to work with several editors. Clearly I have learned from each of them. However, to this point, there are a few to whom I owe much:

- Margaret Quinlin, President and Publisher of Peachtree Publishers. I can't tell you how much your steadfast support and faith in my work has meant to me. Your uncanny ability to see the heart of a story, to lead through just-right questions, and to keep me focused (which is quite a feat) is remarkable. I am a better writer because you are a stellar editor and unmatched friend. Thank you for your calm, kindness, and laughter.

- Lois Bridges, goddess. (That is, goddess—period.) I love how we just start talking about whatever is on our minds and I end up with a book to write. How do you do that? All joking aside, I am grateful for your insightful mind, your gentle spirit, and your passionate beliefs about teaching and learning, teachers and learners, and living with dignity.

- Adrian Peetoom, my first editor. What a standard you set for all others to follow. I am grateful to your keen eye, your sharp mind, and your open heart.

And there are those who have played other roles in this project. My thanks to the keen wit and unmatched talents of Mike Gibbons and John Gayle, who made the videos for this project nothing short of stellar. I watch them and think, "How'd they do that?" Remember, I was there when they shot them, and I'm amazed at the final product. Thanks to you both for your genius and zeal. You are the best.

My thanks also to Ray Coutu for your careful attention to detail, your gentle reminders, your compassion, and your genuine concern for delivering the best to teachers. I am grateful to finally have had the opportunity to work with you. It was long overdue.

A special thanks to my dearest friend, Reba Wadsworth, and the folks from Woodmeade Elementary in Decatur, Alabama, and to Barb Gratsch and the folks from Country Hills Elementary in Coral Springs, Florida.

And finally, I am deeply appreciative of the continuous outpouring of love and support from family members throughout this difficult and trying year: Zachary Laminack, Glenda Laminack, Cindy Flowers, Amanda Jo Cone, Scott Laminack, and my dad, Jimmy. To have this project emerge from the turmoil of this year has been a blessing surpassed only by the grace of your kindness.

Introduction

As a writer and an educator, I have had numerous opportunities to work directly with children and teachers in the study of the craft in my own writing. From that vantage point, I am able to discuss craft with attention to more than just the moves made in the writing. I don't have to make a theory about *why* a craft move was made in my own writing. I know *what* I did, *why* I did it, and *how* to repeat it in another place within the same text or in a future text.

Over the past few years, as I have provided professional development through in-class writing workshops, demonstration lessons, conferences, and other presentations, several teachers have suggested that I make a collection of videos for teachers to share with their colleagues and students. So, I have taken that challenge; a resource bank of videos can be found at **scholastic.com/authorcraft**. *Cracking Open the Author's Craft* is written for teachers and their students as well as for other educators who provide staff development. As a writer and an educator, I am in a position that enables me to give you and your students an inside view of the craft in my own work. My hope is that *Cracking Open the Author's Craft* will give you and your students insight that will help you think more deeply about the art of writing and write with greater control over it.

Who Should Read This Book?

I have written this book to be a flexible resource for educators in various roles. In the section that follows, I address each role.

Teachers

You are the primary audience for *Cracking Open the Author's Craft*. From the beginning, I thought of you as I conceived this project. I envisioned you in your classroom working alongside your students, revealing the moves a writer makes. I thought of you holding these bits of insider knowledge and slipping them in at just the right moments while you work with your children. I imagined you viewing the videos and selecting clips to share with your students in order to give them even more options as writers. *Cracking Open the Author's Craft* is designed to deepen your knowledge of the study of the author's craft and then to be used in segments with your students. The videos enable me to visit your classroom and talk directly with your students.

I open with a read-aloud of my picture-book memoir, *Saturdays and Teacakes*. You could play this first segment for your students as a stand-alone read-aloud or use it as an overview for the launch of a craft study. In the segments that follow the read-aloud, I explain what I mean by audible and visual craft and then identify seven audible craft moves and seven visual craft moves. In the video segments I identify the 14 moves and explain my thinking behind each one, being careful to point out why I made the move. Each of these segments is accompanied by a written lesson that follows a consistent template you can use to explore the craft in other texts. At the end of each written lesson, you will find a short list of other texts that contain additional examples of the featured craft move. I call these books *anchor texts* because they will serve to hold the craft move in the writer's mind. Seeing examples in three to five different books will help writers of any age see the possibilities that can exist for a particular craft move. The anchor texts can become a teaching resource long after the lesson has ended. I would also encourage you to attempt similar moves in your own writing to further the experience for your students. You will find the 14 written lessons on pages 25–55.

I have attempted to make this project very flexible. You could begin with the book and read it as you would any other professional book. You could also begin with the videos, view that first, and then read the accompanying book. You could move between the book and the videos, viewing segments and reading the corresponding text. The video segments can be used to provide examples and background for you before you take the lessons to your students, or you could show the segments to your students as if I am a daily visitor during the study. There is no "right" way to approach this. I developed the project to provide you with as much flexibility as possible. I realize that each of you will need to make this work fit your particular students, in your classroom, within your constraints. This book also contains a section titled "A Workshop to Grow Your Knowledge

Base." This section is designed as a way to deepen the professional knowledge base of those who work with student writers.

Librarians and Media Specialists

Cracking Open the Author's Craft can be an addition to your teacher resource collection. I envision you reading through the book and viewing the videos to help teachers locate other books they could use in the study of the author's craft. At the conclusion of each of the 14 written lessons (pages 25–55) you will find other picture books listed. Each of these anchor texts will contain examples of the craft featured in the lesson. I call them *anchor texts* because they can be used to help writers hold the craft move in their thinking. You can be a resource person to classroom teachers by pulling these anchor texts and having them bundled by lesson. In addition, you will find that the more familiar you become with author's craft in children's books, the more you will notice. Then as you read books with children in the library, you will be able to draw attention to those features in the text that teachers and students have under study in the writing workshop. And you could use the video of my reading *Saturdays and Teacakes* as a read-aloud in the library.

> LUCY CALKINS on the power of learning from authors:
>
> **"I've come to believe... that when I conducted elaborate author studies, immersing my students in a sea of trivial details about my favorite authors, I was probably learning more than were my children.... How much better it would have been had I invited each of my students to find a book that mattered enormously to him or her, and then to search for a second book by that same author, and finally, to put those two books together, asking, 'What does the author tend to do?' and 'Can I borrow any of these techniques in my own writing?'"**
>
> —from *The Art of Teaching Writing*

Literacy Coaches and Staff Developers

I envision you using *Cracking Open the Author's Craft* first to refresh, extend, or refine your own knowledge base. Then, in your role as one who leads teachers toward more finely tuned practice in the teaching of writing, you can use the book and videos as a staff development tool. The videos can be viewed in segments with copies of *Saturdays and Teacakes* at hand. View this with your colleagues, pausing at the close of each segment to return to the text of *Saturdays and Teacakes* for a closer examination of the writing, and then work together to find examples of similar craft in other books as you broaden the professional knowledge base of a faculty. Each lesson includes a short list of other titles that include examples of the craft move featured. Lead an inquiry into how the craft moves in those texts are similar to the move featured in *Saturdays and Teacakes*. Think through the reasons for each craft move in the anchor texts and talk through the notion that a single move could be made for several purposes. In addition, the video segments can be used directly with children as you coach and model lessons in classrooms.

SIMON FRENCH on the influence of reading on writing:

"I read as much as I can. I read books, not to pinch ideas, but to see how other authors write. I read to see how stories are put together, and to see which kind of story appeals to me, and to others— and why."

—from *Lasting Impressions: Weaving Literature into the Writing Workshop* by Shelley Harwayne

This book also contains a section titled "A Workshop to Grow Your Knowledge Base." This section is designed as a way to deepen the professional knowledge base of those who work with student writers. It includes a series of opportunities for delving into picture books with the purpose of becoming more adept at reading like a writer, identifying craft moves and forming theories about why those moves were made, and thinking through ways to lead other writers toward the use of those moves as appropriate. This section includes suggestions to think about and forms to record insights arising from studying the author's craft in picture books. As an instructional leader, you can guide the inquiry into craft with little more than copies of the forms, the videos, copies of *Saturdays and Teacakes*, and copies of the anchor texts.

Principals and Other Administrators

Cracking Open the Author's Craft is a tool you can use to deepen your insights into the teaching of writing. This close study of the craft of one writer will give you greater insights into the possibilities for curriculum and instruction in writing. It will support your work as an instructional leader and enable you to observe the teaching of writing through an informed perspective. *Cracking Open the Author's*

Craft will enable you to pull up alongside a student and have more insightful conversations as you participate in his or her development as a writer. If your role includes staff development, note the comments to literacy coaches and staff developers.

Welcome, Readers

So, dear readers, welcome. Welcome to the close study of craft in my writing. I don't assume for one second that I have all the answers, let alone the correct answers. I have my understandings, my insights, and my notions of craft as they apply to the writing I do. I invite you to explore those insights and understandings. Take from them what you will, and make this book your own. Build your understanding and insights to make your instruction in the writing workshop more tightly focused. Have fun with this. Language is fluid and flexible. Play with it. Try it out. Lead your students toward more efficient and more effective writing. Surely if we think together, we will all be wiser for the effort.

Online Resources at scholastic.com/authorcraft

The webpage is divided into sections that include both video clips and downloadables. Let me briefly explain what you'll find:

Read-Alouds

On your own, you may want to listen to me read my picture book *Saturdays and Teacakes* before you read the book yourself to your students. Or, you can take me right into your classroom (via the videos) and invite me to read the book to your class. If you would like to have a copy of *Saturdays and Teacakes* to share firsthand yourself, you can find it in your public library or you can order it directly from my children's book publisher, Peachtree: **peachtree-online.com**.

Lessons

Watch the videos to add to your knowledge about author's craft before you teach the lessons yourself. Or, again, if you'd prefer, you can use the videos in your classroom and let me share firsthand with your students. You can watch the lessons in any way you choose—one at a time or in clusters. You might like to do a unit of study just on the audible craft lessons, spending a week or two exploring what this means across anchor texts, and then do the same for the visual craft lessons. *Cracking Open the Author's Craft* is completely flexible; use it in the way that makes the most sense for you and your students.

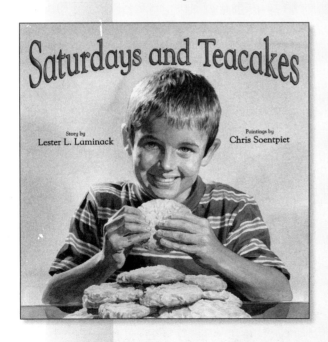

Q&A With Lester

In this section, I share a range of thoughts and ideas that address various aspects of *Cracking Open the Author's Craft* including:

- What's the difference between craft and technique?
- What's the difference between audible and visual craft?
- Why did I use my own book to explain author's craft?
- What can be learned from living with a book?
- How do you get started in your study of author's craft?
- What do we aim to accomplish by teaching author's craft?
- How can we turn to published authors for writing lessons?
- How do kids react to author's craft?
- Is it okay to break the rules?
- How do you help your kids learn the language of author's craft?
- How do you get better at understanding and teaching author's craft?
- How do you refine your understanding of author's craft?

Downloadable Forms and Student Samples

These are ready-to-use forms you can download from the website and print. The five are self-explanatory; read them and you'll know how to use them. They are:

- Noticings from well-loved picture books
- Taking a closer look at a well-loved picture book
- Moving from curriculum to selection of books
- Supporting my students as they grow in their understanding of author's craft
- Finding teaching points in well-loved picture books

You'll also find the book's student samples on the website.

Mammaw Thompson's Teacake Recipe

Toward a Working Definition of Author's Craft

Craft According to Lester

Craft is the art of writing. Craft can be found in those intentional touches each artist layers into his or her work, leaving a "voice print" behind for any reader to find.

Craft has to do with word choice, so a rich and robust vocabulary is an important tool for writers. Writers are typically folks who are enormously taken by words and consume them as listeners and readers in much the same way athletes and dancers consume food to nourish their bodies.

Craft has to do with sound, or what I like to call the music of language, so writers are typically attentive to rhythms and cadence in language when listening and reading. Writers read with an ear for the sound of language, and writers are typically people who read often.

Craft has to do with attention to detail. Writers must be able to tell enough to move the text along. They must also be able to show enough to take the reader/listener along with the story on the same current that tugged at the writer. Writers are attentive folks who take note of the world around them, especially the little things that other people might simply walk right past.

Craft has to do with the placement of words on the page. Writers manipulate print to signal to the reader their intentions regarding pace, tone, intensity, and mood in much the same way a composer uses notations to signal to musicians. They notice how the placement of print and the use of white space can impact the way a reader reads. Writers read with an eye for placement of text and print. And writers write with their reader(s) in mind.

Craft is the intentional use of techniques—including word choice, imagery, sound, rhythm, cadence, the placement of words on the page, use of white space—to create a desired impact upon the reader and to evoke a response from the reader. It is important to note that writers use craft with care. It isn't done randomly or without thought. Writers craft their work with care and purpose. They may want to set a particular mood or evoke certain emotions. They may want to alter the way a reader paces the story or to nudge the reader to increase or decrease intensity or volume in specific spots.

EUDORA WELTY on the influence of reading on writing:

"Learning to write may be part of learning to read. For all I know, writing comes out of a superior devotion to reading."

—from *The Eye of the Story*

When craft techniques are not used thoughtfully, the end result will likely be less than effective. Overusing a craft move or using a technique without thinking through the desired effect can actually distract the reader from making meaning. It is important to read with craft in mind, to learn how writers create their work and to try out the techniques or moves you discover. It is equally important, if not more important, to reflect on *why* the writer used a technique. Knowing *how* to do it is only part of the knowledge needed for more effective writing. Knowing *when* and *why* is also essential. Otherwise, we may see young writers layering in craft moves with a random effect that tends to clutter the writing and take the reader off track.

Writers often begin with a thought, an idea, a spark of inspiration, or a title that develops into a vision for their work, and crafting is part of that vision. This is not to say that vision includes the small details of every craft move. In fact, some of the craft in my writing has become almost intuitive. The more you read with the eyes and ears of a writer, the more the moves of a writer seep into your thinking and become part of the way you use language to communicate more effectively and more efficiently.

But to reach the point where craft is an intuitive aspect of your writing, you begin deliberately trying out the moves of writers you admire. Think of it as watching an athlete or dancer or potter or baker whose work you hold in high regard. When given the chance to watch your "mentor" at work, you "read" his or her moves with focus and attention and a deliberate intention. Later you explore those moves as you try them out. As you do, you might say or think through what you noticed, replaying it in your mind as you attempt to execute the move yourself.

To play out this analogy, consider that each move made by your "mentor" is done for a purpose and not for show; that is, it is not just "decoration." Each move is made by the writer to impact the reader/listener in some way. It may be to build tension. It may be to slow the pace and cause the reader to linger in the moment.

The point is to notice what the writer did. Think about the effect it has on your reading. Think about how the writer did that—can you see how it's done so you can try it too? Think about why the writer did that—what was he or she hoping to accomplish? How many times is it done? Does this number have an impact on the way the text works?

[handwritten margin note: How did what the writer did affect your reading? Every detail is there for a reason.]

Audible Craft and Visual Craft

Katie Wood Ray (1999) has described craft as being both word-level and structural. Word-level craft would include all the language use and the careful, deliberate, and artful choice of words. Structural craft, on the other hand, would include the organizational framework of the work, the way the print lies on the page, and the way a writer uses white space. In addition to thinking of craft in these ways, I like to think of craft also as being either audible or visual.

Audible Craft *[handwritten: — listening to things read aloud]*

Audible craft is what I call the artful use of language that lingers in your ears even after the book is closed. It is part of the "music" in language, the sound print that is left behind in the ear of the readers or listeners. Audible craft is the artful use of language that can be noticed even without seeing the print. To gain a bit of insight into this, take a book you admire and read it aloud to a group of students. Ask them to listen with attention to the language and what the writer may have done on purpose. Ask them to listen and make a mental note of what they notice in the language. As you reach the end and close the book, invite your students to turn and talk with a neighbor or small group and generate a list of all they noticed. Chart these insights and return to the book. Read it aloud a second time, stopping when you come upon anything the group has noticed. At these junctures, ask your students to pose theories about why a writer would make that move. Remember, the noticing and reflecting and thinking are more important than the answer. The more you read and notice these moves in writing, the more you will see patterns of use and purpose. But the truth is, you will not *know* the answer unless you are able to interview the writer. However, it is important to think about what the writer did to cause you to notice. It is also important to think about how and why the writer made that move and caused you to notice. Think about how the move affected you as a reader. Think about what that move did to add to your experience as a reader or listener and how it impacted the meaning you were able to construct. Remember, craft has a purpose; it is not just decoration.

Visual Craft - seeing the text yourself

Visual craft is what I call the thoughtful and artful and planned placement of print on the page. It involves the use of print features like fonts, italics, boldface, and punctuation marks. Visual craft involves using line breaks and white space and manipulating the size of print. The distinguishing factor, in my view, is that visual craft must be *seen* to be noticed, that is, a listener would not know what the writer did to influence the reader's voice.

Lessons for Leading Writers Forward

The following section will present a series of craft lessons using a consistent format or template. These lessons could be done in the writing workshop as needed or in a series with a focus on craft study. You could focus the study through the lens of a single title or with the work of a single author. You could also take the slant of using a set of texts to show that each craft lesson can be demonstrated in several ways.

The Lesson Framework

Each of the craft lessons will be presented using a framework built off the work of Katie Wood Ray. In her book *Wondrous Words* (1999, p. 120) Katie outlines the five parts to reading like a writer.

1. *Notice* something about the craft of the text.

2. *Talk* about it and *make a theory* about why a writer might use this craft.

3. Give the craft a *name*.

4. Think of *other authors* you know. Have you seen this craft before?

5. Try to *envision* using this crafting in your own writing.

Notice the Craft/Name the Craft

Your comments might include these questions and statements:

- What did you notice as I read this aloud?

- What do you notice on this page?

- What has the writer done with the print here?

- How is the white space used differently here?

- What I noticed next was...

- If you are like other kids I've worked with, you may have noticed...

- Many people who write often...

Form a Theory

Your comments might include these questions:

- Why would a writer do this?

- How does this help you as a reader?

- Are there other places in this text where the author has done this?

- When you find other instances of this, how does that affect your theory? Does it make you more certain? Does it nudge you to reconsider?

- Does this help your theory grow? If so, how?

Explore Other Authors

Your comments might include these questions and statements:

- Do we know other writers who do this?

- Let's explore one of these books (anchor texts from class set) and see if we notice any other writers who do this.

- What do you notice in these books?

- Consider your theory and check it in this title. Are both authors doing this for the same reason?

- Is there more than one reason to use this crafting technique? What other possibilities are you thinking of?

For each lesson I recommend anchor texts that highlight the literary element we're exploring and include the literary language that captures the element. In the appendix, you'll find a complete listing of all the anchor texts with bibliographic information so that you can take it to the library and easily pull the titles you might like to share with your students.

Think About Your Own Writing

Your comments might include these questions:

- How would you use this in your writing?

- Can you imagine this working for you?

- Would this work in the writing you are doing now?

This framework is intended to lead student writers toward a life of reading like a writer who notices the ways other writers craft their work and influence their readers. It is my hope that a consistent framework will help student writers develop a habit of mind that includes careful and deliberate artful moves in their own writing.

Getting Ready for Craft Study: Reading Like a Writer

I have heard my friend Katie Wood Ray say that everything we know as writers we know as readers first. I embrace that same thinking and know that my own writing life is greatly influenced by what I read. So I offer this section to lead us toward noticing what writers do, thinking about how and why they do it that way, and what we might do in our own writing.

Learning to Notice What Writers Do

When you read or listen to someone else read, you can hear the music in language. You hear the way the words flow together smoothly. You hear rich, robust description. You hear words that capture your attention and cause you to see an image or feel an emotion. You hear the sounds of noisy words and the soft whisper of quieter ones. You can hear the effect of decisions made by a writer—words, images, alliteration, consonance, metaphors, similes, dialogue, repeated words or phrases or details, and so on. The point is that writers make deliberate decisions that leave a "sound print" on a reader's ear. To read like a writer you must first be aware that writers make these decisions with purpose and care. Next, you have to begin to expect to hear them as you read or listen to the language of the writer.

And remember that writers also craft their work in ways that can be seen. These include such things as changing the font and using punctuation in interesting ways. This visual craft also includes things such as the use of white space and the placement of the print on the page. It also includes the use of italics and bold print and underlining and more. These are all things you can see clearly as you look at the print on the page.

Now, as we begin to take a closer look at the effects of the decisions that writers make, we will try to zoom in and crack open what the writer has done. But, more important, we will make theories about why the writer made these decisions. By thinking about the reasons for decisions and the intentions behind them, we begin to discover the ways we can use the same crafting techniques ourselves. As we begin to listen and look more closely when we read, we will find that the music and art of writing will filter into our thinking through our ears and eyes. And because of that we begin to write with more deliberate intentions, in more artful ways. Now, let's give this a try.

LUCY CALKINS on the importance of knowing a few books very well:

"If one text can be used as an exemplar of many qualities of good writing, we can take the time to read it together for all the wondrous ways in which it affects us, and only then return to it in order to examine the ways in which it embodies particular qualities of writing. What is most important is that we and our students be moved by a book. Only then do we return to the book to ask, 'What did the author do to affect me in these ways?' If _Owl Moon_ is a familiar book to our class, we might look at its lead sentence and those of several other touchstone books during a single mini-lesson. We won't be disembodying those leads or tearing them from their contexts, because if these are touchstone books, members of our classroom community will already know the book. As we discuss the lead, we will be able to talk about how it fits with the whole of the book. Another day, we may notice metaphor, or description, or the sound of words, or dramatic scenes, or treatment of chronological order. As we return to the book again and again, we find ourselves understanding the author's message more deeply, the author's craft more completely."

—from _The Art of Teaching Writing_

Audible Craft Lessons From
Saturdays and Teacakes

The seven lessons that make up this section introduce audible craft

moves I made in *Saturdays and Teacakes*. I will explain the reasons

behind each move so that you and your students can hear how

I made it and, more important, why I made it.

Remember to visit scholastic.com/authorcraft to watch me

read aloud *Saturdays and Teacakes* and demonstrate a lesson on

audible craft study.

Notes: audible craft: repeated words, onomatopoea,
the way words are read (tone/volume)
"row after row of fresh stripes on the lawn"
• descriptions, not explanations. He showed —
didn't tell.

• @ end, ask students to turn+talk about
the things they thought the author
did on purpose to make parts "linger
in their ear" +help them to remember

Audible Craft Lessons

LESSON 1 Repeated Words

"pedal, pedal, pedal"

1. Notice the Craft/Name the Craft

What are some of the things you noticed while listening to the story Lester wrote? One thing you might have noticed as you listened is that Lester uses the words "pedal, pedal, pedal" in several places. Let's call that "repeating a word." Did you hear how he repeats the word *pedal* three times in each place he used it?

2. Form a Theory

Let's think together and make a theory about why Lester does this in his story. How does it help us to make sense as we listen? Why would he use the words "pedal, pedal, pedal" over and over again?

Here are some likely responses:

- The three words together, "pedal, pedal, pedal," help us to see the boy moving his legs, so maybe it is used to help us create an image.

- Repeating the three words several times in the story helps us to see all that he passed along the way to his grandmother's house. Perhaps he is using this to draw our attention to the places he passed along the way.

- It lets us know he had to ride a long way to get there, so we know it was a lot of work. He might want us to know that seeing his grandmother was very important to him. Or perhaps he is also looking forward to doing the work because it makes him feel important to her.

- Using those words helps us to know that he knew the way to his grandmother's house, he knew all the neighbors and streets along the way, and he was safe in that travel.

- Repeating the word three times in several places serves as a transition between the different parts of his trip to his grandmother's house.

3. Explore Other Authors

Can you think of another author who has repeated words? Have we heard this done in any other book we have read? Let's take a look at these books (anchor texts from class set) to see if we notice something like what Lester has done here. Is there another book you know where the author repeats the same word throughout several scenes in a story?

Have books ready for students to explore, revisit, or point out. You could also make this connection explicit, depending upon your intentions and your time.

Click, Clack, Moo: Cows That Type
Written by Doreen Cronin
Illustrated by Betsy Lewin

Click, clack, **moo**.
Click, clack, **moo**.
Clickety, clack, **moo**.

4. Think About Your Own Writing

Now we have some good ideas about how a writer could use this craft. And we have thought through how the craft helps us to make sense of the writing. So, let's begin thinking about how we might use this same craft in our own writing. Read through your work to see if you have any of these same intentions for your writing. Would this craft help your work be more focused? Can you use this craft in your next revision? If not, can you think of work you might do later in which this craft would be a good idea?

In the dialogue, draw out connections between the intentions of any of your student writers and the effect in the examples from professional writers. You could also point to a possibility for writing you are doing as a bridge between the example of a professional writer and the writing your students are doing. If students have difficulty imagining work where this craft could be useful, share some possibilities of your own.

LESSON 2 Repetition of a Specific Phrase
"every Saturday"

I. Notice the Craft/Name the Craft

As we read the story aloud, some of you noticed that Lester uses the words "every Saturday" in several places. Let's call that "repeating a phrase." Did you hear how he repeats the phrase "every Saturday" several times throughout the story?

2. Form a Theory

Let's think together and make a theory about why Lester does this in his story. How does it help us to make sense as we listen? Why would he use the phrase "every Saturday" over and over again?

Here are some likely responses:

- The phrase "every Saturday" shows us that he made this trip each week all summer.

- Repeating the phrase "every Saturday" several times in the story helps us to realize that this visit and all the things that happened each week were very important events in his life.

- It lets us know that he and his grandmother had a routine. They depended upon each other to be there; they were making a tradition between them.

- Repeating the phrase "every Saturday" so many times ensures that we won't miss the importance of the trip. If he had used "every Saturday" only once or twice we might have a different impression of how important the time together was for each of them.

3. Explore Other Authors

Think of books we have read together. Is there another author who has repeated a phrase like this? Have we heard this done in any other book we have read? Let's take a look at these books (anchor texts from class set) to see if we notice a writer repeating a phrase as Lester has done here. Is there another book you know of in which the author repeats a phrase throughout the text?

Have books ready for students to explore, revisit, or point out. You could also make this connection explicit, depending upon your intentions and your time.

The Other Side
Written by Jacqueline Woodson
Illustrated by E.B. Lewis

"That summer..."

In November
Written by Cynthia Rylant
Illustrated by Jill Kastner

"In November..."

Whoever You Are
Written by Mem Fox
Illustrated by Leslie Staub

"...may be different from yours."

The Sunsets of Miss Olivia Wiggins
Written by Lester L. Laminack
Illustrated by Constance R. Bergum

"She didn't move, she didn't even blink, but slowly, quietly, she began to think..."

The Magic Hat
Written by Mem Fox
Illustrated by Tricia Tusa

"Oh, the magic hat, the magic hat! It moved like this, it moved like that!"

4. Think About Your Own Writing

Now we have some good ideas about how a writer could use this craft. And we have thought through how the craft helps us to make sense of the writing. So, let's begin thinking about how we might use this same craft in our own writing. Read through your work to see if you have any of these same intentions for your writing. Would this craft help your work be more focused? Can you use this craft in your next revision? If not, can you think of work you might do later in which this craft would be a good idea?

In the dialogue, draw out connections between the intentions of any of your student writers and the effect in the examples from professional writers. You could also point to a possibility for writing you are doing as a bridge between the example of a professional writer and the writing your students are doing. If students have difficulty imagining work where this craft could be useful, share some possibilities of your own.

LESSON 3 Proper Names (street names, names of neighbors, etc.)

"Thompson Street," "Bells Mill Road,"
"Mrs. Cofield's house," "Mrs. Grace Owens's house,"
"Chandler's Phillips 66."

I. Notice the Craft/Name the Craft

While listening to the story Lester wrote, you noticed that he gave the names of streets and neighbors and stores that he passed along the way. Let's call that "using proper names to make it real." You could listen again and write directions from his house to his grandmother's house.

2. Form a Theory

Let's take a minute to think about why Lester does this in his story. How does it help us to make sense as we listen? Why would he include so many proper nouns throughout his memoir? Let's talk about that and make a theory.

Here are some likely responses:

- The names of people, places, and streets help us to see Lester making his way across town.

- When Lester gives us the names of the streets, it helps us to make a map in our minds. Since we know this is a memoir, and we know that means this story is nonfiction, we could find a map of Heflin, Alabama, and follow his route.

- Using the names of the people who live in the houses he passes lets us know that he knew the people along the way to his grandmother's house. It lets us know that those people also knew him. That gives us the feeling that he is safe and being looked after because he knows he could stop for help if he needed it.

- Naming the people who live in each house also lets us know that his mother and grandmother could call to check on his progress through the trip if they got worried. Again, that helps us to know that he is safe.

- Naming places like "Chandler's" and "The Bank of Heflin" and the old oaks in Mr. White's yard helps us to know he has places he passes each Saturday. He takes the same route each week, and he has familiar places to stop along the way. Again, it helps to give us a sense of the routine and ritual of this journey.

3. Explore Other Authors

Can you think of another author who has used proper names? Have we heard this done in any other book we have read? Let's take a look at these books (anchor texts from class set) to see if we notice something like what Lester has done here. Is there another book you know of in which where the author uses proper names?

Have books ready for students to explore, revisit, or point out. You could also make this connection explicit, depending upon your intentions and your time.

Come On, Rain!
Written by Karen Hesse
Illustrated by Jon J. Muth

"Miz Grace," "Miz Glick," "Miz Vera," "Liz," "Rosemary," "Jackie-Joyce"

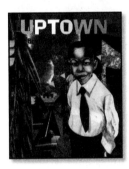

Uptown
Written and illustrated by Brian Collier

"Metro-North train," "Harlem River," "the Ruckers"

4. Think About Your Own Writing

Now we have some good ideas about how a writer could use this craft. And we have thought through how the craft helps us to make sense of the writing. So, let's begin thinking about how we might use this same craft in our own writing. Read through your work to see if you have any of these same intentions for your writing. Would this craft help your work be more focused? Can you use this craft in your next revision? If not, can you think of work you might do later in which this craft would be a good idea?

In the dialogue, draw out connections between the intentions of any of your student writers and the effect in the examples from professional writers. You could also point to a possibility for writing you are doing as a bridge between the example of a professional writer and the writing your students are doing. If students have difficulty imagining work where this craft could be useful, share some possibilities of your own.

LESSON 4 Brand Names

"Red Diamond Coffee," "Golden Eagle Syrup," "Blue Bonnet Margarine," "Frigidaire"

I. Notice the Craft/Name the Craft

As you listened to the story, some of you noticed that Lester includes the brand names of the coffee and margarine and syrup that his grandmother used in her kitchen. Let's call that "using brand names." Do you remember the names "Red Diamond" and "Golden Eagle," "Blue Bonnet," and "Frigidaire"?

2. Form a Theory

Let's return to those places in the story. Listen again as I read. This time think about why Lester does this in his story. How does it help us to make sense as we listen? Why would he use the brand names of these things?

Here are some likely responses:

- Let's remember that this is a memoir, a true story about Lester when he was a boy. With that in mind, he may be using the specific brand names just because those are the products his grandmother used in her kitchen.

- The specific brand names also help us to know something about the place. The names "Red Diamond" and "Golden Eagle" are not national brands we see in commercials. So, they must be from his town or area. Or they could be products that were used in that time. The names help us get a sense of when and where the story is happening.

- The brand names are very specific details that give the story a sense of truth. They help us to believe that the story really happened. They help us to get a clearer picture of what is in the kitchen.

3. Explore Other Authors

Do we know any other book in which the author has used the specific brand names of products? Is there a book in our classroom library with that craft in it? Let's take a look at these books (anchor texts from class set) to see if we notice another writer using specific brand names as Lester has done here.

Have books ready for students to explore, revisit, or point out. You could also make this connection explicit, depending upon your intentions and your time.

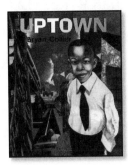

Uptown
Written and illustrated by Brian Collier

"The Apollo Theater," "Van Der Zee photograph," "the Ruckers," "the Boys Choir of Harlem"

4. Think About Your Own Writing

Now we have some good ideas about how a writer could use this craft. And we have thought through how the craft helps us to make sense of the writing. So, let's begin thinking about how we might use this same craft in our own writing. Read through your work to see if you have any of these same intentions for your writing. Would this craft help your work be more focused? Can you use this craft in your next revision? If not, can you think of work you might do later in which this craft would be a good idea?

In the dialogue, draw out connections between the intentions of any of your student writers and the effect in the examples from professional writers. You could also point to a possibility for writing you are doing as a bridge between the example of a professional writer and the writing your students are doing. If students have difficulty imagining work where this craft could be useful, share some possibilities of your own.

LESSON 5 Honoring Speech

"We best clear these dishes away and get out in that yard before it gets too hot." "You go on ahead to the car house. . . I'll be out directly." "You cool off and rest a spell. I'm gonna make us a bite to eat."

I. Notice the Craft/Name the Craft

Several of you noticed while listening to the story that Lester uses different language when his grandmother speaks. You might have noticed as you listened that Lester uses words like these when his grandmother is talking: "We best clear these dishes away and get out in that yard before it gets too hot." "You go on ahead to the car house. . . I'll be out directly." "You cool off and rest a spell. I'm gonna make us a bite to eat." Let's call this "honoring the speech of a character."

2. Form a Theory

Let's think about why a writer would use one way of talking as the narrator and another way of talking for one of the characters. Think about that for a moment, and let's put our ideas together and make a theory about why Lester does this in his story. How does it help us to make sense as we listen?

Here are some likely responses:

• The language of his grandmother is different from the way we talk today. Maybe he does this to help us know this was a long time ago. In that case, "honoring the speech of a character" helps to establish the time frame for the setting.

• We know this is a true story, a memoir. So, when Lester uses a different way of talking for his grandmother, we could be fairly certain that he is trying to capture and honor the language she used.

• When Lester uses different language for the narrator and his grandmother it helps us to see that he is a writer who pays attention to his characters. He is using his grandmother's language, her dialect, to help us know her better. It is a way of building the character.

3. Explore Other Authors

Now let's think about other authors we have studied. Can you think of another author who honors the speech of his or her characters? Have we heard different language in the voice of a character in any other book we have read? Let's take a look at these books (anchor texts from class set) to see if we notice a writer honoring speech as Lester has done in *Saturdays and Teacakes.*

Have books ready for students to explore, revisit, or point out. You could also make this connection explicit, depending upon your intentions and your time.

The Other Side
Written by Jacqueline Woodson
Illustrated by E. B. Lewis

"I live over yonder," she said, "by where you see the laundry. That's my blouse hanging on the line."

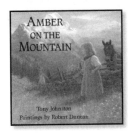

Amber on the Mountain
Written by Tony Johnston
Illustrated by Robert Duncan

"You can't build a road here. Folks will roll clean off it, like walking up a wall." "You can do almost anything you fix your mind on."

4. Think About Your Own Writing

Now we have some good ideas about how a writer could use this craft. And we have thought through how the craft helps us to make sense of the writing. So, let's begin thinking about how we might use this same craft in our own writing. Read through your work to see if you have any of these same intentions for your writing. Would this craft help your work be more focused? Can you use this craft in your next revision? If not, can you think of work you might do later in which this craft would be a good idea?

In the dialogue, draw out connections between the intentions of any of your student writers and the effect in the examples from professional writers. You could also point to a possibility for writing you are doing as a bridge between the example of a professional writer and the writing your students are doing. If students have difficulty imagining work where this craft could be useful, share some possibilities of your own.

LESSON 6 Sound Effects (onomatopoeia)

"criiick-craaack-criiick-craaack"

I. Notice the Craft/Name the Craft

When I read the story, several of us noticed the sounds of the glider and the sound of the wind whistling in Lester's ears as he zoomed downhill on his bike. Many of us have used sound words in our writing as well. Let's call this "using sound effects." Did you notice, though, that Lester used these sound effects very, very sparsely? It's true—he used *whoosh* only once and *criiick-craaack-criiick-craaack* is used only twice.

2. Form a Theory

Let's think together and make a theory about why Lester does this in his story. How does it help us to make sense as we listen? Why would he use the words *whoosh* and *criiick-craaack-criiick-craaack* in this story?

Here are some likely responses:

- The "whoosh" helps us to realize that Lester is zooming downhill very fast. He is moving so fast we can hear the wind rushing past his ears. Perhaps he lets us hear the sound of the wind so we can feel that rushing, fast-moving sense of zooming downhill with him.

- The sound of the glider, *criiick-craaack-criiick-craaack*, is a slow and easy sound that gives us the sense of spending time without rushing. It helps us to see Lester's grandmother as a gentle and patient woman who is just waiting for him to arrive. It seems as if it is a comforting sound to Lester.

- Using the sound effects in only two or three places helps us to notice them more. If Lester had included sounds in several places, we might not have paid attention to them as much. Perhaps he was very selective in his choice to get us to notice the two places or two sounds that were most significant to his memory of the trip.

3. Explore Other Authors

Can you think of another author who uses sound effects? Does that writer use them frequently or in only one or two places? Does it seem as if that writer is using sound effects for the same reasons we think Lester is using them? Let's take a look at these books (anchor texts from class set) to see if we notice other writers using sound effects in the same way or for a different purpose.

Have books ready for students to explore, revisit, or point out. You could also make this connection explicit, depending upon your intentions and your time.

Roller Coaster
Written and illustrated by Marla Frazee

"Clickity, clackity. Clickity, clackity."... "WHOOSH!"

Mr. George Baker
Written by Amy Hest
Illustrated by Jon J. Muth

"Tappidy-boom.
Tappidy-boom.
Tappidy-boom-boom-tap."

Achoo! Bang! Crash! The Noisy Alphabet
Written and illustrated by Ross MacDonald

"BOO! BING! BUMP BASH! BOP!"
(Note: The book is nothing but onomatopoeia.)

4. Think About Your Own Writing

Now we have some good ideas about how a writer could use this craft. And we have thought through how the craft helps us to make sense of the writing. So, let's begin thinking about how we might use this same craft in our own writing. Read through your work to see if you have any of these same intentions for your writing. Would this craft help your work be more focused? Can you use this craft in your next revision? If not, can you think of work you might do later in which this craft would be a good idea?

In the dialogue, draw out connections between the intentions of any of your student writers and the effect in the examples from professional writers. You could also point to a possibility for writing you are doing as a bridge between the example of a professional writer and the writing your students are doing. If students have difficulty imagining work where this craft could be useful, share some possibilities of your own.

LESSON 7 Figurative Language (metaphors, similes, personification)

"…a shower of tiny pebbles…," "…sunlight poured in like a waterfall…," "…mower choked on mouthfuls of wet grass…," "…the dew-pearls were gone…," "…gobbled mine down like a hungry dog…"

I. Notice the Craft/Name the Craft

Many of us heard Lester use imagery as he gave rich description of his memories from those Saturdays. Let's jot down a few examples of the imagery Lester creates using figurative language. Several of us noticed these phrases: "…a shower of tiny pebbles…," "…sunlight poured in like a waterfall…," "…mower choked on mouthfuls of wet grass…," "…the dew-pearls were gone…," "…gobbled mine down like a hungry dog…" Let's call that "using imagery to capture the reader's imagination." Lester does this using similes and metaphors, and in one or two places he includes personification.

2. Form a Theory

Now let's return to a few of those places and listen again. This time think about why Lester uses imagery in his story. How does it help us to make sense as we listen? Why would he use metaphors and similes and personification in this story?

Here are some likely responses:

• Lester uses imagery to compare what is there with something else. For example, when he describes the sunlight coming through his grandmother's kitchen window as a waterfall, it catches our attention. We pause a moment and think of that image. We imagine a waterfall of sunlight pouring through. Perhaps, then, a writer uses a simile to catch our attention and draw our focus. Or perhaps he wants us to think of an ordinary thing in a different way.

• As we read along there were times when we paused on a second or third reading to take a closer look at the art. Remember when Lester described the dew drops on the grass as "dew pearls," and we paused to look at the illustration. Perhaps writers use metaphor and simile to cause us to pause and think or to draw our attention to a detail. Drawing our attention to the dew drops on the grass could be a way of letting us know that he began mowing the grass early in the morning.

• Think about the place where Lester says the mower "choked on mouthfuls of wet grass." We know a mower doesn't actually have a mouth, so Lester must have a reason for using that image. We do know what it means to choke on something and we do know that if you put too much in your mouth you might choke. So, by comparing the machine mowing grass to a live creature eating, Lester helps us to imagine how the machine might sometimes shut down. Perhaps, then, a writer uses personification to help us make more meaning from the writing.

3. Explore Other Authors

Let's take a few moments now to think of books we have read or listened to. Do we know other writers who use imagery well? Let's take a look at these books (anchor texts from class set) to see if we notice something like what Lester has done here. Is there another book you know of in which the writer uses imagery such as metaphor and simile and personification?

Have books ready for students to explore, revisit, or point out. You could also make this connection explicit, depending upon your intentions and your time.

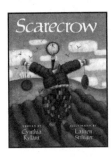

Scarecrow
Written by Cynthia Rylant
Illustrated by Lauren Stringer

"They ignore his pie-pan hands and the button eyes and see..." "He has watched a spider work for hours making a web like lace. He has seen the sun tremble and the moon lie still."

The Barn Owls
Written by Tony Johnston
Illustrated by Deborah Kogan Ray

"...and leaves the barn through a bale of light." "...long snakes sunned and split their skins like chaff and left."

In November
Written by Cynthia Rylant
Illustrated by Jill Kastner

"Without their leaves, how lovely they are, spreading their arms like dancers. They know it is time to be still." "In November, at winter's gate, the stars are brittle. The sun is a sometime friend. And the world has tucked her children in, with a kiss on their heads, till spring."

4. Think About Your Own Writing

Now we have some good ideas about how a writer could use this craft. And we have thought through how the craft helps us to make sense of the writing. So, let's begin thinking about how we might use this same craft in our own writing. Read through your work to see if you have any of these same intentions for your writing. Would this craft help your work be more focused? Can you use this craft in your next revision? If not, can you think of work you might do later in which this craft would be a good idea?

In the dialogue, draw out connections between the intentions of any of your student writers and the effect in the examples from professional writers. You could also point to a possibility for writing you are doing as a bridge between the example of a professional writer and the writing your students are doing. If students have difficulty imagining work where this craft could be useful, share some possibilities of your own.

CRACKING OPEN THE AUTHOR'S CRAFT

Visual Craft Lessons From
Saturdays and Teacakes

The seven lessons that make up this section introduce visual craft

moves I made in *Saturdays and Teacakes*. I will explain the reasons

behind each move so that you and your students can see how

I made it and, more important, why I made it.

Remember to visit **scholastic.com/authorcraft** to watch me

read aloud *Saturdays and Teacakes* and demonstrate a lesson on

visual craft study.

Notes : visual craft

LESSON 1   Italics

The mother's speech (*You stop and look both ways when you get to Chandler's...*), the sound of the wind whistling in Lester's ears (*whoosh*), the sound of the glider (*criiick-craaack-criiick-craaack*), the grandmother's speech (*Come on into this house. Let's have us a bite to eat.*).

1. Notice the Craft/Name the Craft

As we moved back through the book taking a closer look at the printed language, one thing we saw was that Lester used italics in several places. Italics are used when his mother or grandmother talk and when a sound effect is used. Let's call that "using italics to show sound."

2. Form a Theory

Now let's think together and make a theory about why he does this in his story. How does it help us as readers? What does it help us to notice?

Here are some likely responses:

• Italics are used when his mother and his grandmother have something to say. Perhaps writers can use italics to show speech.

• We noticed there are no quotation marks used when Lester uses italics for the talk of his mother and grandmother. And he doesn't talk with them, it is as if he is remembering what they said. Perhaps the italics in this case show talk from his memory.

• The italics are also used to show sounds of the wind in his ears and the sounds of the glider. Those are sounds he would have to remember since he is writing about a time when he was nine or ten years old. Perhaps the italics are used to show any remembered sound.

3. Explore Other Authors

We have seen many authors use italics. Let's think a bit about a few books we know where italics have been used. Can you remember a book in which the writer used italics to show sounds from the past? Have we seen this done in any other book we have read? Let's take a look at these books (anchor texts from class set) to see if we notice something like what Lester has done here.

Have books ready for students to explore, revisit, or point out. You could also make this connection explicit, depending upon your intentions and your time.

The Sunsets of Miss Olivia Wiggins
Written by Lester L. Laminack
Illustrated by Constance R. Bergum

"She remembered a Sunday afternoon…"
(Alternating scenes are written in italics to signify a flashback or memory in Miss Olivia's mind.)

The Horned Toad Prince
Written by Jackie Mims Hopkins
Illustrated by Michael Austin

"Que pasa, senorita?" "Yo tengo mucho hambre."
(All Spanish words are written in italics and are keyed to a Spanish-to-English word list on the back end papers.)

Jake's 100th Day of School
Written by Lester L. Laminack
Illustrated by Judy Love

"Mr. Thompson said he had a *superrific* surprise…"
"Tomorrow will be *101* days of school." "But, it wasn't the *100th* day anymore." (Italics are used to signify a stressed or emphasized word.)

4. Think About Your Own Writing

Now we have some good ideas about how a writer could use this craft. And we have thought through how the craft helps us to make sense of the writing. So, let's begin thinking about how we might use this same craft in our own writing. Read through your work to see if you have any of these same intentions for your writing. Would this craft help your work be more focused? Can you use this craft in your next revision? If not, can you think of work you might do later in which this craft would be a good idea?

In the dialogue, draw out connections between the intentions of any of your student writers and the effect in the examples from professional writers. You could also point to a possibility for writing you are doing as a bridge between the example of a professional writer and the writing your students are doing. If students have difficulty imagining work where this craft could be useful, share some possibilities of your own.

LESSON 2 Stretching Out the Print

"Pedal… pedal… p-e-d-a-a-l-l-l…,"
"criiick-craaack-criiick-craaack"

I. Notice the Craft/Name the Craft

As we moved through the book taking a closer look at the printed language, we saw that Lester stretched out a few words using extra spaces and/or adding in letters. Stretching the words is done in only three places, and each time it makes us read the words differently. Let's call that "stretching a word to change the sound."

2. Form a Theory

Now let's think together and make a theory about why Lester would stretch words in his story. Does it help us as readers? What does it help us to notice? How does it make us read the language differently?

Here are some likely responses:

• Lester includes several sets of "pedal, pedal, pedal," but only one set has extra space between the words and stretches the last word, *pedal* (*p-e-d-a-a-a-l-l-l*). That last pedal has dashes between each letter and Lester has added two extra *a*'s and two extra *l*'s so in the book it looks like this: *"Pedal… pedal… p-e-d-a-a-l-l—"* When we read the text around that spot, we notice that he had just zoomed down hill and this is the first place Lester has a big hill to pedal up. Perhaps the spacing between the three words and the added ellipses show he is pedaling more slowly. But the last *pedal* (*p-e-d-a-a-a-l-l-l*) in that set is more stretched and causes us to read the word with an exaggerated sound as if we are straining to make it up the hill.

• Perhaps a writer stretches a word to change the way we say it when we read it aloud.

• Perhaps a writer stretches a word to show emphasis, to help us feel excitement or stress or other emotions.

3. Explore Other Authors

We have seen other writers stretch words. Let's think of books we know in which words have been stretched like this. Have we seen this done in any other book we have read? Let's take a look at these books (anchor texts from class set) **to see if we notice something like what Lester has done here.**

Have books ready for students to explore, revisit, or point out. You could also make this connection explicit, depending upon your intentions and your time.

"Hurty Feelings"
Written by Helen Lester
Illustrated by Lynn Munsinger

"You hurt my f*eeeee*lings!" (used to exaggerate the emotion and stretch the word)

Roller Coaster
Written and illustrated by Marla Frazee

"S-l-o-w-l-y the train . . ." "AND GOES ALL-L-L-L-L-L-L-L-L-L THE WAY AROUND." "WHEEEEEEEEEEEEEEEEEEE!" (used to exaggerate the emotion.)

The Recess Queen
Written by Alexis O'Neill
Illustrated by Laura Huliska-Beith

". . . ringity, zingity, YESSSSSS!" (used to exaggerate the emotion)

4. Think About Your Own Writing

Now we have some good ideas about how a writer could use this craft. And we have thought through how the craft helps us to make sense of the writing. So, let's begin thinking about how we might use this same craft in our own writing. Read through your work to see if you have any of these same intentions for your writing. Would this craft help your work be more focused? Can you use this craft in your next revision? If not, can you think of work you might do later in which this craft would be a good idea?

In the dialogue, draw out connections between the intentions of any of your student writers and the effect in the examples from professional writers. You could also point to a possibility for writing you are doing as a bridge between the example of a professional writer and the writing your students are doing. If students have difficulty imagining work where this craft could be useful, share some possibilities of your own.

LESSON 3 Stacking Words

"One…

two…

three…

four driveways and one last turn to the left."

1. Notice the Craft/Name the Craft

Taking a closer look at the printed language, we saw that Lester stacked the words vertically like a tower instead of writing them in a horizontal line the way we expect to see written language. Let's call this "stacking words." Lester does this in only one spot in the story.

2. Form a Theory

Now let's try reading it together and see how it sounds when we read it as Lester wrote it. Then we'll try reading it as if he had written it on a horizontal line, like most sentences. We can see if it makes a difference in how it sounds. Then we can make a theory about why he does this in his story. Does it help us as readers? Does it make a difference in how we read the language aloud? What does it help us to notice?

Here are some likely responses:

- There is only one place in the whole story where the words are stacked. Each of the words is followed by ellipsis points. That usually means to slow down and hold the sound at the end of the word and signals that more is coming. Perhaps he does this to make us slow down as we read. So, maybe writers stack words to change the pace of our voice in reading.

- The stacked words are like little driveways. They come one after the other and look the way driveways would look on a map. Maybe Lester does this to make us think of the way driveways are spaced apart and not so close together. Perhaps writers stack words to help readers get the picture.

3. Explore Other Authors

Can you remember a book in which the writer stacks words? Have we seen this done in any other book we have read? Let's take a look at these books (anchor texts from class set) to see if we notice something like what Lester has done here.

Have books ready for students to explore, revisit, or point out. You could also make this connection explicit, depending upon your intentions and your time.

Uptown
Written and illustrated by Brian Collier

"Uptown
is
weekend shopping
on
125th Street."

The Recess Queen
Written by Alexis O'Neill
Illustrated by Laura Huliska-Beith

"Katie Sue!
A teeny kid.
A tiny kid.
A kid you might scare
With a jump and a 'Boo!'"

Come On, Rain!
Written by Karen Hesse
Illustrated by Jon J. Muth

"Quietly,
    while Momma weeds,
        I cross the crackling-dry path past..."

Jake's 100th Day of School
Written by Lester L. Laminack
Illustrated by Judy Love

"A hundred buttons.
    A hundred marbles.
        A hundred rubber bands.
            And sailing all around his head,
                a hundred paper planes..."

4. Think About Your Own Writing

Now we have some good ideas about how a writer could use this craft. And we have thought through how the craft helps us to make sense of the writing. So, let's begin thinking about how we might use this same craft in our own writing. Read through your work to see if you have any of these same intentions for your writing. Would this craft help your work be more focused? Can you use this craft in your next revision? If not, can you think of work you might do later in which this craft would be a good idea?

In the dialogue, draw out connections between the intentions of any of your student writers and the effect in the examples from professional writers. You could also point to a possibility for writing you are doing as a bridge between the example of a professional writer and the writing your students are doing. If students have difficulty imagining work where this craft could be useful, share some possibilities of your own.

LESSON 4 Sentence Fragments

"She was waiting for me. No one else. Just me."
"She was waving to me. No one else. Just me."

I. Notice the Craft/Name the Craft

As we moved back through the book taking a closer look at the printed language, we saw that Lester used sentence fragments in a couple of places. Let's call this "the intentional use of a fragment."

2. Form a Theory

Now let's think together and make a theory about why he does this in his story. What does it do to our reading? How does it help us as readers? What does it help us to notice?

Here are some likely responses:

• The fragments are part of a context so the meaning is not lost. It does not leave us confused. But it does make us read it differently. The fragments cause us to pause longer, to stop and start, putting more silence between each segment: "She was waiting for me. [stop and pause] No one else. [stop and pause] Just me. [stop, end of page]." Perhaps one way writers use fragments is to create a specific rhythm in the language.

• In the spot where Lester uses the fragments, the scene is slowing down. The first sentence in the paragraph is rather long—24 words. This long sentence is followed by the cluster containing these fragments: "She was waiting for me. No one else. Just me." So, in this paragraph we move from 24 words to five words to three words and finally to two words. It is as if the journey is slowing down and coming to a stop when Lester arrives at his grandmother's house. So, perhaps a writer can use fragments to slow time in the story.

3. Explore Other Authors

Take a moment to think about the books we have read together and the books you have read on your own. Can you think of authors who have used sentence fragments for some effect in their writing? Can you remember a book in which the writer used fragments to slow time in the story? Or a writer who used fragments to change the rhythm in the language? Have we seen this done in any other book we have read? Let's take a look at these books (anchor texts from class set) to see if we notice something like what Lester has done here.

Have books ready for students to explore, revisit, or point out. You could also make this connection explicit depending upon your intentions and your time.

The Recess Queen
Written by Alexis O'Neill
Illustrated by Laura Huliska-Beith

"Katie Sue!
  A teeny kid.
  A tiny kid."

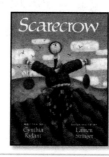

Scarecrow
Written by Cynthia Rylant
Illustrated by Lauren Stringer

"A liking for long slow thoughts. A friendliness toward birds."

Mr. George Baker
Written by Amy Hest
Illustrated by Jon J. Muth

"Our books are green, and his lips sound out the letters. Real slow. But his fingers fly across his knees. Like a big old drum."

Jake's 100th Day of School
Written by Lester L. Laminack
Illustrated by Judy Love

"A hundred buttons.
  A hundred marbles.
    A hundred rubber bands.
      And sailing all around his head,
        a hundred paper planes..."

4. Think About Your Own Writing

Now we have some good ideas about how a writer could use this craft. And we have thought through how the craft helps us to make sense of the writing. So, let's begin thinking about how we might use this same craft in our own writing. Read through your work to see if you have any of these same intentions for your writing. Would this craft help your work be more focused? Can you use this craft in your next revision? If not, can you think of work you might do later in which this craft would be a good idea?

In the dialogue, draw out connections between the intentions of any of your student writers and the effect in the examples from professional writers. You could also point to a possibility for writing you are doing as a bridge between the example of a professional writer and the writing your students are doing. If students have difficulty imagining work where this craft could be useful, share some possibilities of your own.

Visual Craft Lessons

LESSON 5 Parentheses

"You go on ahead to the car house. (That's what Mammaw called the garage.)... Look in the Frigidaire (that's what she called her refrigerator)...."

I. Notice the Craft/Name the Craft

In returning to the book for a closer look at the written language, we noticed that Lester uses parentheses to set off a note of explanation. The parentheses are used when he needs to add a bit of detail. Let's call this "using parentheses to add an explanation."

2. Form a Theory

Now let's think together and make a theory about why Lester does this in his story. Does it help us as readers? What does it help us to notice? Does it make a difference in how we read the language?

Here is a likely response:

* Lester uses parentheses to give more details about a word his grandmother used. When she says "car house," Lester explains that it means the same as "garage." In another place, his grandmother says "Frigidaire" and Lester used the parentheses to explain that this means the same as "refrigerator." Perhaps writers can use parentheses to elaborate in places where the meaning is not clear. Or perhaps writers can use parentheses to explain when the language of one of the characters is unclear.

3. Explore Other Authors

We have seen many authors use parentheses. Let's think a bit about a few books we know in which parentheses have been used. Can you remember a book in which the writer used parentheses to show extra detail or to elaborate? What other ways have writers used parentheses? Have we seen this done in any other book we have read? Let's take a look at these books (anchor texts from class set) to see if we notice something like what Lester has done here.

Have books ready for students to explore, revisit, or point out. You could also make this connection explicit, depending upon your intentions and your time.

Dog Eared
Written and illustrated by Amanda Harvey

"I went back downstairs (eating some horrible peppermint creams along the way) and went straight to bed."

4. Think About Your Own Writing

Now we have some good ideas about how a writer could use this craft. And we have thought through how the craft helps us to make sense of the writing. So, let's begin thinking about how we might use this same craft in our own writing. Read through your work to see if you have any of these same intentions for your writing. Would this craft help your work be more focused? Can you use this craft in your next revision? If not, can you think of work you might do later in which this craft would be a good idea?

In the dialogue, draw out connections between the intentions of any of your student writers and the effect in the examples from professional writers. You could also point to a possibility for writing you are doing as a bridge between the example of a professional writer and the writing your students are doing. If students have difficulty imagining work where this craft could be useful, share some possibilities of your own.

Visual Craft Lessons

LESSON 6 Dashes to Add an Afterthought

"We carefully lifted the circles onto a cookie sheet and put them in the oven to bake—375 degrees for fifteen minutes."

1. Notice the Craft/Name the Craft

Another visit to the book lets us zoom in on the printed words and notice that Lester uses a long dash to add information to a sentence. It is almost as if he forgot something and decided to add it on. The dash is used when he adds a note to let us know how long the cookies needed to stay in the oven and how hot the oven had to be. You could also call this move "using a dash to add detail."

2. Form a Theory

Now let's think together and make a theory about why Lester does this in his story. How does it help us as readers? What does it help us to notice? Does it cause us to read the language differently?

Here are some likely responses:

- The dash is used at the end of a complete thought to add some more detail. That detail could have been included without the dash, but in this way it gets your attention. Perhaps writers use dashes to draw our attention to a detail.

- Lester gives us the procedure for preparing the teacakes. Then, as he describes how the circles are cut and lifted and placed on the pan, he tells us to put them in the oven. It is almost as if he forgot to tell us how hot the oven has to be or how long the cookies have to bake. So, he adds those details with a dash. Perhaps writers use a dash to give the feeling of adding on a forgotten idea.

3. Explore Other Authors

We have seen many authors use dashes. Let's think a bit about a few books we know that contain dashes. Can you remember a book in which the writer used a dash to show a forgotten detail or to draw our atten-tion to a detail? Have we seen this done in any other book we have read? Let's take a look at these books (anchor texts from class set) to see if we notice something like what Lester has done here.

Have books ready for students to explore, revisit, or point out. You could also make this connection explicit, depending upon your intentions and your time.

What You Know First
Written by Patricia MacLachlan
Illustrated by Barry Moser

"Tell them to take the baby—he won't care."
"She cried when we sold the farm—The baby, in her arms, reached up to touch her tears."

Mr. George Baker
Written by Amy Hest
Illustrated by Jon J. Muth

"...when I'm crossing lawns—his and mine— and he's always there..."
"What holds them up—suspenders!"

In November
Written by Cynthia Rylant
Illustrated by Jill Kastner

"...to give thanks for their many blessings— for the food on their tables and the babies in their arms."

4. Think About Your Own Writing

Now we have some good ideas about how a writer could use this craft. And we have thought through how the craft helps us to make sense of the writing. So, let's begin thinking about how we might use this same craft in our own writing. Read through your work to see if you have any of these same intentions for your writing. Would this craft help your work be more focused? Can you use this craft in your next revision? If not, can you think of work you might do later in which this craft would be a good idea?

In the dialogue, draw out connections between the intentions of any of your student writers and the effect in the examples from professional writers. You could also point to a possibility for writing you are doing as a bridge between the example of a professional writer and the writing your students are doing. If students have difficulty imagining work where this craft could be useful, share some possibilities of your own.

LESSON 7 Extra Line Spaces

"Those fifteen minutes seemed to last forever.

Are they ready, Mammaw?
Not yet, buddy.

Are they ready now, Mammaw?
Not yet, buddy. Let's give 'em
a little bit longer.

Are they ready yet, Mammaw?
I reckon they might be."

I. Notice the Craft/Name the Craft

During our journey back through the book, taking a closer look at the printed language, we noticed that Lester included extra spaces between the short paragraphs in which he is asking whether the cookies are ready. He tells us this little exchange takes 15 minutes, and the extra spacing helps us see the passing time. Let's call this "using extra space to make time pass slowly."

2. Form a Theory

Now let's think together and make a theory about why he does this in his story. How does it help us as readers? What does it help us to notice? Does it make us read the language differently?

Here is a likely response:

• Lester places an extra line space between each paragraph. That extra line space causes us to pause a little longer before moving on to the next paragraph when we read. Perhaps writers use spacing to slow the reader down and to show the passage of time.

3. Explore Other Authors

Let's think about a few books we know in which the writer uses extra line spaces to make time pass more slowly. Can you remember a book in which the writer used spacing in this way? Have we seen this done in any other book we have read? Let's take a look at these books (anchor texts from class set) to see if we notice something like what Lester has done here.

Have books ready for students to explore, revisit, or point out. You could also make this connection explicit, depending upon your intentions and your time.

My Lucky Day
Written and illustrated by Keiko Kasza

"So the fox got busy.

He collected twigs.

He made a fire.

He carried water."

4. Think About Your Own Writing

Now we have some good ideas about how a writer could use this craft. And we have thought through how the craft helps us to make sense of the writing. So, let's begin thinking about how we might use this same craft in our own writing. Read through your work to see if you have any of these same intentions for your writing. Would this craft help your work be more focused? Can you use this craft in your next revision? If not, can you think of work you might do later in which this craft would be a good idea?

In the dialogue, draw out connections between the intentions of any of your student writers and the effect in the examples from professional writers. You could also point to a possibility for writing you are doing as a bridge between the example of a professional writer and the writing your students are doing. If students have difficulty imagining work where this craft could be useful, share some possibilities of your own.

So, Now What? Moving Beyond This Study

So, now you have taken a very close look at one book to examine the craft of one writer. Does this mean that you now know all the ways a writer can use craft? Well, of course it doesn't. In fact, we have only begun to examine what writers do. Each of these ways of crafting writing is a very simple technique to try in your own writing. However, writing well isn't as simple as picking up a technique here and there to layer into your work. The key is to begin reading differently. As a writer, you will read with an eye for how the author uses the white space and manipulates the print. As a writer, you will read with an ear for how the author uses language to make music and evoke images and emotion in the reader. When you notice and begin to think about how the writer accomplished that move or made that happen in your mind, don't forget to also give a lot of thought to *why* the writer did it. Knowing why is just as important as knowing how. Knowing why, or at least thinking about how the craft move affects you as a reader, helps you use the same or similar techniques thoughtfully and purposefully. In short, noticing what the writer did, paying attention to how it was done, and thinking about why the move was made will help you create more artful writing.

As teachers we can begin by revisiting the books in our classroom libraries. This time we will read them with a writer's eyes and ears, looking for the art of writing tucked away like treasures to be unearthed. Here is a guide to taking a fresh look at well-loved picture books that hold the potential for dozens and dozens of mini-lessons.

Craft Study

Craft Across Genres and Topics

Craft is like a river flowing across a continent—the water respects no borders arbitrarily drawn on a map. It flows through nations, into and out of states and counties and towns. It overflows its banks and spills into the low-lying valleys through the countryside. Craft flows through written language and respects no borders arbitrarily created by categories for literature. It flows through genres and across topics in service to the writer whose decisions are purpose-driven.

Although our primary example in this project, *Saturdays and Teacakes,* is a memoir, each craft move and each lesson generated from those moves could be repeated in other genres and/or topics. As I see it, the limitation on craft is set by the author's purpose. This is why it is essential to move beyond noticing, naming, and trying a craft move. As others have suggested, it is essential that we take the time to stop and carefully think through *why a writer would use that particular craft move.* Knowing *when* and *how* to use a craft move is critical. In this respect, you could say that craft is *purpose-driven.*

If you examine a dozen texts representing a range of genres, you will find examples of craft in each. In each you can zero in on the function of that craft move and note that the craft is something that can be applied for similar purposes in other genres as well. In fact, you may find it helpful to take a small stack of picture books representing several genres. Read through the set, looking for craft moves that

> LUCY CALKINS on the importance of reading and rereading:
>
> **"Whatever else we do with a touchstone book, we will most certainly reread it. When he was asked 'How do you learn to write?' Hemingway answered, 'Read *Anna Karenina*, read *Anna Karenina*, read *Anna Karenina*.'...** **Only when we read and reread a dearly loved poem or story can the text affect us so much that it affects even our writing."**
>
> —from *The Art of Teaching Writing*

thread across several titles, and take note of your findings. The point is that a craft study can be done within a single genre or across several genres and will lead your students toward more artful and controlled writing.

What Do We Hope For?

As we move toward more focused study of the craft of writers, we should expect to see two specific outcomes. First, children will begin to read differently. As students begin reading like writers, we will notice the language of craft work filtering into the classroom vocabulary. As they read with attention to how and why writers craft their work, the music and art of writing will filter into their ears and eyes. This will lead to the second expected outcome: children will begin to write with more vision, more intentional moves, and more carefully and artfully crafted work.

JOAN DIDION on the importance of dialogue:

"Dialogue, as much as anything else, reveals the character to the writer and ultimately to the reader. I don't have a very clear idea of who the characters are until they start talking."

—from *Shoptalk: Learning to Write with Writers* by Donald Murray

Examining Craft in Student Writing

Take a look, a close look, at the writing of Steven Norwalk, who was six years old at the time this story was written. First, it is significant to know that when I met Steven, he viewed himself as a writer. He kept a writer's notebook (a 3-inch three-ring binder). He had an ongoing 65-page draft of an alternate ending to the first Harry Potter book. It was, of course, 65 pages of a six-year-old's sprawling manuscript on white three-hole-punch notebook paper, but it was a focused, sustained, self-initiated text. And that's just one of the things he had in his notebook.

When I met Steven, I was a visiting author and writing consultant at his school, Country Hills Elementary in Coral Springs, Florida. It was not my first visit there, so the staff and many of the children knew me and had built up my visit as a big deal.

Shortly before my trip, I received an e-mail from my friend Barb Gratsch, who was at that time a literacy curriculum specialist at the school. Barb let me know she had a special request. It seems Steven had decided that as a writer I would not want to eat lunch with just anyone; rather, I should spend that time in the company of another writer—yes, you know he was the writer he had in mind. Who could resist that invitation? So, I graciously accepted and looked forward to it.

That day at lunch I not only met a charming, precious 6-year-old child, I also shared lunch with a confident and focused writer. I fully expect to see his name in publication some day. Keep an eye out for him—Steven Norwalk. It's a writer-kind-of-name, don't you think?

Steven showed me his writer's notebook and asked to see mine. I keep a green notebook with a little gold moose embossed on the cover. (FYI—Field Journal, Homestead Publishing, P. O. Box 193, Moose, Wyoming 83012, 307-733-6248, ISBN-0-943972-16-7.) These are my *favorite* notebooks and I have used them for years. They are incredibly ordinary; the pages are a cream-colored paper with a matte finish and have just a bit of texture. That matters because I am left-handed and do not like to write on slick paper because the ink tends to smear. I don't know what he expected, but Steven seemed disappointed with this rather plain and benign notebook in which almost everything was written in cursive. He didn't say much, he just flipped through the pages as I sat quietly and waited.

Then I asked if I could see his notebook. He handed it over proudly and I turned the pages with great interest. I commented on the volume and variety of work in his notebook and asked what he was currently working on. Steven grinned and

F. SCOTT FITZGERALD on style and the influence of other writers:

"By style I mean color.... I want to be able to do anything with words: handle slashing, flaming descriptions like Wells, and use the paradox with the clarity of Samuel Butler, the breadth of Bernard Shaw and the wit of Oscar Wilde, I want to do the wild sultry heavens of Conrad, the rolled gold sundowns and crazy-quilt skies of Hichens and Kipling as well as the pastelle [sic] dawns and twilights of Chesterton. All that is by way of example. As a matter of fact I am a professional literary thief, hot after the best methods of every writer in my generation."

—from *The Notebooks of F. Scott Fitzgerald*, edited by Matthew J. Bruccoli produced a copy of his most recent draft—"Seahorse Soup." I held the story in my hands and read the title aloud. "That's a clever title," I said. "I'm wondering what this is about. Do you mind if I read it aloud?" Steven granted permission and I read through the piece silently once, then aloud. I was taken by his craft and control.

Now that you have a sense of who this young writer is, let's take a look at the text on page 61, which he had just completed for my visit. Zoom in and see what you notice. Read it aloud to let your ears capture the music of his language, then return to see what your eyes notice that your ears cannot.

JOAN DIDION on the influence of other writers:

"When asked what writer has had the greatest influence on her writing she replied: I always say Hemingway, because he taught me how sentences worked. When I was fifteen or sixteen I would type out his stories to learn how sentences worked.... A few years ago when I was teaching a course at Berkeley, I reread *A Farewell to Arms* and fell right back into those sentences. I mean they're perfect sentences. Very direct sentences, smooth rivers, clear water over granite, no sinkholes."

— from *What If? Writing Exercise for Fiction Writers* by Anne Bernays and Pamela Painter

Seahorse Soup

Once upon a time, in the bluest of the ocean, lived a seahorse who loved to cook. He never made up a recipe befor, so for once he will try it! "I will name it sea horse soup," said seahorse. "What will I need? How about some cod, chickin broth, samon & goldfish.

So off he went to the fish market. down one Ile and up another down one eile and up another. Soon he found what he needed. Then he went back to his cave, took out a pot and was ready to start.

"I wonder how goldfish will taste, only one way to find out" Plop! He dropped the goldfish in the pot! Now some cod. The he dropped the samon in the pot. The he put some parmashon cheese on all of them.

The he cooked the samon, goldfish and cod. When they were done, he dumed them in the bowl with the chicken broth. When he tasted it...

...YUCK!

A year later he made it againe and it tasted...

AWESOME!

by Steven Norwalk, first grade, Country Hills Elementary, Coral Springs, Florida

Here are some things that captured my attention:

- The lead establishes a clear setting and introduces both a character and the genre.

- Setting: "Once upon a time, in the bluest of the ocean..."

- Character/Genre: "lived a seahorse who loved to cook. He never made up a recipe before, so for once he will try it!"

In these brief words we can hear how Steven, a six-year-old boy, has arrested the rhythm and cadence in the music of story language. We hear in his words the ability to echo that music and capture it with his pencil. We know the story is set in a time past, takes place in the ocean, and features a seahorse who cooks. That lets us know the piece is fiction or fantasy.

No one speaks in normal conversation using words like, "Once upon a time in the bluest of the ocean there lived a seahorse..." Can you imagine one of your adult friends *saying* "In the quietest of neighborhoods there lives a teacher who loves to read..." I rather doubt any of us have *ever* heard that sort of language in ordinary speech.

On the other hand, almost all of us will have heard similar language read aloud or we have read it ourselves. So, how would a six-year-old boy—any six-year-old child—come to use such language in his writing? Clearly the music of written language has been played on the instrument of the voices of the significant adults in his life. As those significant adults read aloud and told stories to him, Steven tuned in so that his ears arrested the rhythm of that music. It is a part of him; it is not contrived or forced. It is not fake or overdone. It is artful and well placed; it is balanced and musical. It is craft.

In the excerpt below, notice how Steven artfully moves the story along by repeating the phrase—"down one Ile and up another down one eile and up another."

"So off he went to the fish market. down one Ile and up another down one eile and up another. Soon he found what he needed. Then he went back to his cave, took out a pot and was ready to start."

In much the same way I repeat "pedal, pedal, pedal" in *Saturdays and Teacakes* to move the plot along and take the reader along on the journey to my grandmother's house, young Steven moves the plot along through a quick pace, keeping the reader focused on the topic—making the soup—without getting bogged down in the extraneous details of what is on the shelves in the market. He understands the *purpose* of the move. He demonstrates his understanding of *how* to execute the move and he does so in an artful way. It is craft.

Now zoom in on his ending and notice how he builds tension with the use of ellipses and creates emphasis and meaning with bold capital letters.

> "When he tasted it...
>
> ...YUCK!
>
> A year later he made it againe and it tasted...
>
> AWESOME!"

In his original, handwritten copy you would see that "...YUCK! A year later he made it agine and it tasted..." is written on a page by itself. And you would see that "AWESOME!" stands alone on the last page. Clearly Steven realizes the power of timing in his writing. That is something he has learned through his ears. He has heard stories read aloud and stories told where the voice builds tension and excitement with intensity and pacing. He has learned this through his eyes. He has seen books with bold capital letters. He has seen words standing alone on a page. He has seen and heard the impact of those features of text on the voice of a reader. And now he has brought those insights to his own writing. He is using what he knows as a listener and as a reader to control what another reader will do with his written language. He is writing in an artful way. It is craft.

A Sample From a Kindergarten Writer

Now let's consider another piece written by a five-year-old attending the same school. I was given this sample a couple of years before I met Steven. I was working with the staff at Country Hills, and our focus was on looking closely at the writing of young children to learn more about what to notice. I had been asked to meet with a group of teachers who would each bring a few writing samples. We had transparencies made of each piece and we studied the collection as a group. As each sample was projected for all to see, the teachers and

I talked through what we noticed in each child's work. Our focus was on what we saw as strengths to build on, points to celebrate, opportunities for instruction, and points to ponder as teachers.

However, for the purposes of this project, let's zero in on the craft work in the piece on page 65. I find it helpful to read the piece aloud, to really listen to the voice and the music of the piece.

After a close look and listen, I am drawn to these specifics:

Note how the author draws attention to the beauty of the sunset by offering contrasting perspective—"I was riyt in the Howtiell nekst to the watr I got a Butfull vayw but thar wear peple that waer riyt on the sand they head the best voww." Her inclusion of a contrasting perspective is evidence that she can manipulate point of view to make her point stronger and her meaning more clear.

Also notice how the two different spellings for *beautiful* help the reader to know how these words should be read aloud. The first spelling—*buyootful*—stretches out the word to exaggerate the sounds and places greater emphasis on the spectacular sunset. The second spelling—*butfull*—is a match to her typical pronunciation and does not bring the same emphasis. Her manipulation of spelling and print to govern the reader's pronunciation of the word *beautiful* is evidence of her sense of craft. She shows a sensitivity to the sound of language and an understanding of craft as a way to use sound to draw attention to and emphasize the meaning in her writing.

Through both of these moves we are able to see control in her writing. We see deliberate moves made for effect. In short, she is crafting her written language in much the same way she would manipulate her oral language to draw attention and create emphasis.

As with Steven's "Seahorse Soup," this young writer shows an understanding of the *function* of craft. She demonstrates that she not only knows *how* to use craft moves in her writing but that she also understands *why* she is doing them. It is clear that she understands a basic premise many of us miss in a craft study—craft is purpose-driven.

FRAN LEBOWITZ on reading your work aloud and crafting the sound of language:

"In conversation you can use timing, a look, inflection, pauses. But on the page all you have is commas, dashes, the amount of syllables in a word. When I write I read everything out loud to get the right rhythm."

—from *Shoptalk: Learning to Write with Writers* by Donald Murray

Hawayes Sunsets.

One ningt in Hawiye thar
was a Buyootfull
sun set by the sea
and I was riyt in the
Howtiell nekst to the
watr I got a Butfull
vayw but thar wear
peple that waer riyt
on the sand they head
the best voww

A Sample From a Fifth-Grade Writer

Several years ago, I was working with the fifth-grade teachers and students at Woodmeade Elementary School in Decatur, Alabama. I used George Ella Lyon's poem, "Where I'm From," which is included in her book on writing poetry (1999, *Where I'm From: Where Poems Come From.* Spring, TX: Absey & Company, p. 3) along with Marie Bradby's picture book *Momma, Where Are You From?* (2000, *Momma, Where Are You From?* Orchard) to demonstrate how writers can approach the same topic in two different formats yet have a similar structure. Each author tells a life story—her own story. George Ella does it in a poem. Marie does it as a picture book. Yet, the structure is very similar. I made that structure visible for the children in the fifth-grade classrooms that day. I invited them to try the structure for themselves. On page 67 is a poem from one young man in one of those classes. His name is Chris.

The thing that struck me most when I first read Chris's poem aloud was the way that he so closely captured the rhythm and cadence of George Ella's poem. You will have to read her poem aloud, then read his. You will hear it. I have even read a stanza of hers then a stanza of his alternating back and forth between them and it sounds like one poem. It is as if she were sitting next to him reading in a whisper, filling his ears with the music of her language. He not only echoes the music of her language but also captures the basic structure of her poem, repeating the words, "I am from..." and "From..." at the beginnings of each line. Notice also how he so gracefully moves from the bigger picture of neighborhood, street, driveway, and house to the smaller details—"games, humongous chairs, and a crimson candle that smells like pine" and then zooms in to his room, then to books, and to favorite foods before pulling back the lens to place everything in a broader perspective—memories, church, family, love.

Chris, like the two student writers featured above, has demonstrated his understanding of audible and visual craft. He has tuned his ear to the music of poetry and has captured it with his own voice and mirrored it with his pen. He has crafted his writing.

Chris, where are you from?

I am from a quiet neighborhood, an orange house on
   Bedford Street, and three cars in the driveway
From a house full of games, humongous chairs, and a
   crimson candle that smells like pine.

I am from a room that is nice and neat, baby pictures
   on the wall, and a dresser full of trophies.
From walls of ruby paint, wallpaper filled with roses, and
   a bed that puts you right to sleep.

I am from paper back books, trips to the library, and
   stories from three little Bibles.
From Wilbur in <u>Charlotte's Web</u>, <u>The Three Little Bears</u>,
   and mom helping me.

I am from hot buttered biscuits, grilled cheese, and baby
   back ribs.
From blueberry ice cream and cornbread made from
   scratch.

I am from a world of memories, a house full of
   happiness, and journeys in my mind.
From a church that prays for one another, a family that
   loves me, and that's where I'm from.

A Workshop to Grow Your Knowledge Base

This section is intended as a support to the professional development of one teacher reading this book alone or of a group of teachers working together in a focused study group. I will include several forms that can be utilized to focus attention on the use of picture books as a tool in the study of author's craft. This section could be used in a self-directed study or under the leadership of a literacy coach or staff developer. I hope you find this is a way of extending your knowledge base and refining the study of craft in your writing workshop.

Defining Craft

It is important to begin thinking about a definition of craft as we move toward thinking about ways to teach it. Using a common definition across classrooms can help us to become more focused and consistent in our work.

Try This

Take a few moments to write a definition of craft that would be appropriate to share with your students. How would you explain what craft is? What examples would you pull from books to show what you mean? How will you help your students come to understand the purpose of craft in writing?

If you are working in a group, share your thinking. Push one another to be more specific, to offer examples, and to explain thinking. Work from the individual responses to generate a set of possibilities for your teaching. Then read through what others have said about craft and pull support for your teaching as you find it.

What Have Others Said About Craft?
Toward a Definition

The study of craft in writing has become an important part of instruction in the writing workshop. Craft, sometimes called author's craft or writer's craft, has been discussed and studied by writers for many years.

As early as 1938, Donald Murray was studying craft.

"...I was fourteen years old, I knew I wanted to be a writer, and I discovered there were books that taught the publishing writer's craft, not the correctness I was taught in school but the art that allowed a story to rise from the page and be heard." (Murray, 1996, p. 156)

In more recent years as the writing workshop has gained momentum, our focus on craft has sharpened, and many educators have recognized that the study of craft yields more efficient and more artful writing. At this point it would be useful to state what we mean by "craft" in writing.

Katie Wood Ray helps us clarify the term (Ray, 1999).

"...In my work alongside other teachers during the past few years, I have learned that it helps to just go straight to this, to defining what we mean by craft and then to work back out of that understanding and into thinking about how to help students read like writers so that they can see craft for themselves, both in the texts that writers publish and in the things that writers say about their processes. (p. 25)

"My dictionary defines craft as a special skill or art, and that definition will work just fine to help us understand the craft of writing. A writer's craft is a particular way of doing something; it's a knowledge a writer has about *how* to do something. (p. 25)

"For the purpose of organizing classroom study, I have found it helpful to think about studying the craft of writing in two major categories. In one category I lump all the things there are to learn from writers about the craft of their 'office work'—where they get ideas, how they do research, how they get response to drafts, how they set up their offices. In the other category I lump all the things there are to learn about how writers craft actual drafts, how they make the writing 'come out' in powerful texts. (p. 26)

"Crafted places in texts are those places where writers do particular things with words that go beyond just choosing the ones they need to get the meaning across. The 'special skill or art' to writing is knowing more and more of these 'particular things' to do with words. This is what helps writers write well when they have an audience in mind, it helps them garner attention for what they have to say, and it helps them find that place beyond meaning where words *sing* with beauty." (p. 28)

Mem Fox views craft as a vehicle for bringing power to writing.

"I'm anxious about the power, or lack of it, in school writing. Power is about being able to craft a piece of writing so effectively that its purpose is achieved. *Craft* means being able to put those understandings into practice. *Craft* means struggle in that battlefield between the brain and the hand until the best possible draft is achieved.... Such power doesn't come from nowhere. It comes from practicing writing for real reasons. It comes from having read powerful writing. It comes from having been taught, and I mean taught, the basic skills of spelling and punctuation in the context of real writing events. Those who write well have more power and therefore more control over their lives." (Fox, 1993, pp. 20–21)

These comments may spark the question of whether craft is something that writers simply acquire or whether it is something that can be taught. William Sloane contends:

"[c]raftsmanship is the use of tools and materials in order to make something in a seemly and economical fashion. For instance, it is *not* craftsmanship to decide to build a table and buy half the lumberyard and have, when the table is finished, approximately eighty or ninety oddly shaped pieces of wood lying around on the floor and hundreds of bent nails and screws and great piles of sawdust. Craftsmanship does indeed carry with it this element of economy of materials. And when it is appropriate to the object being constructed (in this case a book), it acts to enhance. . . . Mastery starts with words. . . . So while it may not be possible to teach people much about writing, it is possible for some people to learn something about *how* to write." (Sloane, 1979, pp. 26–31)

Donald Murray shared these thoughts:

"The writer will never learn to write, for the craft of writing is never learned, only studied. But the teaching writer can share the continual apprenticeship to craft with the writer's students. And they will be motivated together to practice pounceability, lured on by each new surprise. One of the most exciting things about writing is the fact that surprise is much more than idea. Surprise is experience in seeing the vision of the text come clear. Surprise is felt in the working out of the order, direction, proportion, and pace of the text. Surprise is the reward for the line-by-line crafts of revision and editing—the writing keeps saying what we do not expect to hear." (Murray, 1989, p. 10)

To further the conversation, let's consider Ursula LeGuin's thoughts on craft.

"Once we're keenly and clearly aware of these elements of our craft, we can use and practice them until—the point of all the practice—we don't have to think about them consciously at all, because they have become skills.

"A skill is something you know how to do.

"Skill in writing frees you to write what you want to write. It may also show you what you want to write. Craft enables art.

"There's not luck in art. There's the gift. You can't earn that. You can't deserve it. But you can learn skill, you can earn it. You can learn to deserve your gift. . . .

"I think an awareness of what your own writing sounds like is an essential skill for a writer. Fortunately it's one quite easy to cultivate, to relearn, reawaken.

"A good reader has a mind's ear. Though we read most of our narratives in silence, a keen inner ear does hear them. Dull, choppy, droning, jerky, feeble: These are all faults in the sound of prose, though we may not know we hear them as we read. Lively, well-paced, flowing, strong, beautiful: these are all qualities of the sound of prose, and we rejoice in them as we read. And so good writers train their mind's ear to listen to their own prose—to hear as they write." (LeGuin, 1998, pp. xi, 19–20)

So, to teach our students *how* writers do their work we have to make the moves visible. So, when we zero in on finished writing we will be looking closely at the *how*, but we must also consider the *why* behind each move made. First, writers (both student writers and professional writers) must be readers. William Zinsser notes:

> "The race in writing is not to the swift but to the original… Make a habit of reading what is being written today and what has been written by earlier masters. Writing is learned by imitation. If anyone asked me how I learned to write, I'd say I learned by reading the men and women who were doing the kind of writing *I* wanted to do and trying to figure out how they did it. But cultivate the best models."
> (Zinsser, 2001, p. 35)

In order to grow our students into being more efficient and effective writers, to help them gain greater insight and control over the craft of writing, we want to make a habit of reading, though not just reading to enjoy the story or reading to gain insight and construct meaning. We want to help students (and ourselves) learn to read with a writer's ears and eyes.

Katie Wood Ray suggests that we should define what we mean by craft and then move into texts of all sorts with that definition guiding our reading.

> "The moves writers make in texts are not generally ones we can have explained to us, unless we have the opportunity to crawl inside a writer's head as he or she is drafting. We have to work backwards from what we see in a finished text to what we imagine the writer did to make it come out that way."
> (Ray, 1999, p. 28)

I like to think of it as going on a tour of homes with an architect. The architect will notice features in the building, in the structure, in the "craftsmanship" that will go unnoticed by most other visitors. The architect will have insight into the underlying support, the way that support system works to keep the building stable, and the reason it was designed that way.

Read a book with a writer, or read as a writer, and you will notice similar things in texts. You will see *what* the writer did, *how* it was done, and you will be able to surmise *why* it was done that way. From that knowledge you will be able to consider making use of a move or technique or skill in your own writing as it is appropriate to your purpose as a writer. And that is, in my view, the application of craft. And it is the primary reason I decided to write this book and speak directly to you and your students with the video collection at scholastic.com/authorcraft. I realize you cannot *know* the *why* behind the moves you are able to notice in what you read unless you are able to "crawl inside a writer's head as he or she is drafting." Well, I can do that for you. I can take one of my own books and identify those moves I made with deliberate intentions. I can speak those intentions and begin to demystify the craft of writing.

Let's turn to thinking about the ways we can help our students make the most of a study of craft. Once again, I'll pull from the thinking of several writers and educators who have shared their thoughts on the teaching of craft.

What is craft?

Katie Wood Ray:

Searching for answers to questions such as these:

- Where do writers get their ideas?

- How do they do research?

- How do they get response to their drafts?

- How do they set up their offices
  (space and time for writing)?

And it is

- a knowledge a writer has about *how* to do something.

William Sloane:

- the use of tools and materials in order to make something in a seemly and economical fashion

Mem Fox:

- the struggle in the battlefield between the brain and the hand until the best possible draft is achieved

What can we do to help our students learn the craft of writing?

Mem Fox:

- Help students to care about writing by making it real.

- Give my students opportunities for real responses from people they admire.

- Create situations in which students always own the investment in their writing.

- Be sensitive to the social nature of writing, and the vulnerability of writers.

- Demonstrate and encourage writing for fun and huge enjoyment and power.

- Respond after publication as well as before.

- Help to develop powerful writing so that my students can control their own lives.
  (Fox, 1993, pp. 21–22)

So, let's begin reading children's literature with new eyes and ears. On page 76 you'll find some suggestions from Katie Wood Ray to guide your move toward reading like a writer.

The Five Parts to Reading Like a Writer

1. Notice something about the craft of the text.

2. Talk about it and make a theory about why a writer might use this craft.

3. Give the craft a name.

4. Think of other texts you know. Have you seen this craft before?

5. Try to envision using this crafting in your own writing.

(Ray, 1999, p. 120)

Digging Into Children's Literature

It is important to become very familiar with children's literature as you work toward a reading/writing workshop classroom. A study of craft will be more powerful and effective if we, as teachers, have well-developed knowledge of literature available to children. While the primary example cited in this book is a memoir (*Saturdays and Teacakes*), we need to have a working knowledge of a wide range of books representing a variety of topics, formats, genres, and styles.

Try This

Choose five picture books you have come to treasure. Read each one silently, then read it aloud. Think about each book, using the checklist on pages 78–79. Then use that checklist and the form on page 80 to make notes as you revisit your favorites. These notes will be used in other opportunities for getting to know the books in your collection.

Taking a Closer Look at a Well-Loved Picture Book

Examine a well-loved picture book to find out how a favorite author may lead your writers to explore new possibilities.

How does this author move the piece from start to finish?

- Follows the clock moving hour by hour through the day
- Moves day by day through the week
- Moves month by month through the year
- Moves season by season through the year
- Moves birthday by birthday through the life of a character
- Follows the sun moving morning to noon to afternoon, and so on
- Follows a sequence of events in order of their happening
- Follows the movement of a character or event through geography (up the block, across town, up the mountain, over the river)

How does this author use punctuation?

- To slow the pace
- To move the story along faster
- To show the reader how the language should sound
- To show the reader when to turn the volume up or down

How does this author use font size and style?

- To show the reader when voice changes
- To show the reader when to stress a word
- To show the reader where there is a shift in time
- To show the reader where there is a shift in mood
- To show the reader where there is a shift in tone

How does this author provide support and elaboration?

- To explain a procedure or event

- To define a potentially difficult word

- To offer an example

- To say something another way for clarity or emphasis

- To make a connection for an unknown audience

▶ *More for you to consider when revisiting a favorite book:*

How does this author reveal the mood of the character(s)?

How does this author use words in interesting ways that could lead my writers to explore new possibilities in their writing?

How does this author zip through time to move past less important details?

How does this author slow time down to stretch small moments and draw attention to more-significant details?

How does this author lead the reader to anticipate an upcoming event?

Noticings From Well-Loved Picture Books

➤ How does this author move the piece from start to finish?

_____

_____

➤ How does this author use punctuation?

_____

_____

➤ How does this author use font size and style?

_____

_____

➤ How does this author provide support and elaboration?

_____

_____

➤ How does this author reveal the mood of the character(s)?

_____

_____

➤ How does this author use words in interesting ways that could lead my writers to explore new possibilities in their writing?

_____

_____

➤ How does this author zip through time to move past less important details?

_____

_____

➤ How does this author slow time to stretch small moments and draw attention to more-significant details?

_____

_____

➤ How does this author lead the reader to anticipate an upcoming event?

_____

_____

Take the information you have pulled from your stack of books and begin to think about it as raw material for your teaching. Choose one book from your stack and read it through once again with your noticings in mind. Use the form on page 83 to follow the thinking of reading like a writer.

1. What do I see this author doing?

In this column, jot a quick note that will serve to remind you of the move the writer has made. If you find it helpful, include the language of the writer from the source text.

2. Why does the author do this? What job does it do for the reader?

In this column, jot down your thoughts on the function of the craft move. Remember, making a theory about *why* a writer makes this move is as important as recognizing the move. If your students fail to recognize why the move is made, they will most likely lack control of the move in their writing—even if you have successfully shown them *how* to make the move. Remember that the *thinking* in this part is important. So, be sure in your teaching that you include your students in the process of thinking about *why* a writer does this.

3. Have I seen this in other writing? Where?

In this column, make note of any other examples you can locate. You want to be able to demonstrate that a craft move can work across topics, genres, and forms. Have those texts available for support as your students begin thinking about crafting their own writing.

4. What can we call it so we will notice it in the work of others and use it ourselves?

The point in this column is to keep it simple. Just call the move something that makes sense. Remember that your goal is to make this accessible to children.

The purpose of giving the move a name is to make the move easier to discuss. A name is like a handle that enables a writer to carry the ideas around, talk about them, and try them out in clean and efficient ways. In this way, we can also talk about the move when we see it again in other work or in our own.

5. How could I try this in my writing? Try it out.

Now, brainstorm ways you might try this same move in your own writing. Make brief notes in this column. Note the piece of writing you might try this in. Mark the piece as an example you could use in your teaching.

6. How could I lead my writers to try this?

In this last column, think through the opportunities you could take advantage of in your instruction (mini-lesson possibilities, conferring, mid-workshop interruptions, small-group work, and so on).

Finding Teaching Points in Well-Loved Picture Books

What do I see this author doing?	Why does the author do this? What job does it do for the reader?	Have I seen this in other writing? Where?	What can we call it so we will notice it in the work of others and use it ourselves?	How could I try this in my writing? Try it out.	How could I lead my writers to try this?

Moving From Curriculum to Selection of Books

Coming to know children's literature is valuable in itself; however, our purpose here is to generate instructional support for the curriculum. The close study of children's literature done here should produce material to support mini-lessons, conferring, and small-group work within the writing workshop. In an attempt to move our thinking in that direction, I invite you to take the stack of books you have been working with and think about them from another perspective.

Try This

First, think about the unit of study you are about to begin. Use the form on page 86 to list any of the teaching points you plan to include in your instruction. Now, place one of those in each cell under the column headed *What am I planning to teach?*

Begin with your first teaching point and move across the row. Think about the books in your stack (or in your personal collection). Which authors come to mind as the best possible mentors for your students? List specific titles for each author. Now dig into those books and lift out examples of the author's work that will lead your students to new insights about the *how* and *why* of an author's craft.

With this information, you have the essence of *what* to teach. So now you have to begin thinking about *how* you will use this information. What are the options for connecting my students to the work of the author(s) in this example? Here are some possibilities:

- Launch an author study.

- Lift out examples of the same craft move from several authors.

- Demonstrate in your own writing how you used this move. Show the connection between the "mentor author's" work and your work. In doing this, you create a bridge between the work of student writers and the work of professional writers.

- Study the craft moves of this writer in a single book.

- Study one craft move across several books and/or authors.

As you think through the curriculum and what you have to teach, there will be books to make each craft move more concrete for your students. Coming to know a stack of books as intimately as you know your best friends will put you in a position where each author represented in your stack becomes a mentor to the writers in your community.

Moving From Curriculum to Selection of Books

What am I planning to teach?	Which author could be a mentor for this teaching? Which titles will I need?	Examples from this author's work that will lead my writers to new possibilities	How can I best mentor my writers to this author?

Looking Closely at Student Writing

At this point, you may find it helpful to return to the writing samples from children. (See pages 61, 65, and 67.) Read through that section one more time. Then, bring in a few samples from children you know.

Try This

Read through the writing samples you have collected. It is helpful to read them aloud once you have read through them silently. Listen for the audible craft they may have included. Make note of what you notice, and try to identify the source of the influence they are writing under. Look for places where you have an opportunity to lead them toward new moves. You will see evidence of that in places where your students appear to be approximating the craft moves of the mentor writers in your collection. You will gain additional insights about their intentions and understandings from the comments they make while you are conferring with them.

With this information at hand, begin thinking about the connections you could make between the work your student writers are moving toward and the craft moves you have already identified in the work of the professional writers in your collection. Use the questions below to think through how you could make that connection more concrete. Record your thinking using the form on page 89.

I. What are my writers approximating? Growing toward?

In this cell, note one thing your student is working toward or use this to plan for the group and look for patterns across the writing samples of the class.

2. What evidence do I have from their work?

In this cell, pull samples of language from your students' writing to document what you are noting in the first cell.

3. What can I demonstrate to extend those attempts?

At this point, think through your options for possible demonstrations including, but not limited to, examples from your own writing, examples from other students, examples from literature under study.

4. Which author can be my co-teacher in this work? Which titles will be my best examples?

Return to the notes from your close study of picture books and identify those authors and titles that could be used to support. Make note of these in the appropriate cell. Flag the corresponding segment of text in the book to have it ready for your teaching.

5. What examples can I offer to provide a range of options?

Collect samples of language from the anchor text to show the move you wish to feature.

Our focus was on what we saw as strengths to build on, points to celebrate, opportunities for instruction, and points to ponder as teachers.

You may also find it useful to plan your workshop mini-lessons using the form on page 90. My colleague Reba Wadsworth adapted the form from the work of Lucy Calkins and her collegues at Teachers College Reading and Writing Project.

Supporting My Students as They Grow in Their Understanding of Author's Craft

What are my writers approximating? Growing toward?	What evidence do I have from their work?	What can I demonstrate to extend those attempts?	Which author can be my co-teacher in this work? Which titles will be my best examples?	What examples can I offer to provide a range of options?

Planning for Instruction

Unit of Study: Date:

(One) Teaching Point:

Teaching Method: ❑ demonstration   ❑ guided practice   ❑ inquiry   ❑ explain and give examples

Materials Needed:

Connection (1 minute): *Writers, yesterday we were working on...*

Teach (4–5 minutes): *Today I want to teach you how...*

Active Engagement (4–5 minutes): *So, writers, let's try this... Partner 1 turn to Partner 2 (Turn and Talk)... Stop and Jot...*

Link (1 minute): *So, writers, today when you are writing and you...(restate the teaching point)*

A Closing Word From Lester—A Plea for Common Sense

I have a passion for language and literacy. Ask anyone who knows me, and you'll find out quickly that I love to talk with people. I love the music in language and playing with words. I love to read and become lost in a book, to live among the characters and the action. I love to get caught up in the fascination of a well-crafted work of nonfiction. I adore the crafting of written language, working with words to communicate with others I may never meet. But more than all this, being in the presence of children who are learning with the zest of hungry chicks is nothing short of exhilarating. If you are reading this book and viewing the accompanying videos, it is a safe gamble that you are one of those who love language and working with children as well.

However, the increasing demands for raising test scores and teaching more content in each year of school and pushing harder and harder on younger and younger children is something that has begun to rob teachers of the joys of teaching. And worse yet is the impact upon children. We are seeing the very definition of what it means to be a child changing before our eyes. And who is the beneficiary of all this? Are our children the ones to experience a more significant quality of life? Are our children the ones who fall in love with learning, with language, with living in a world with an open sense of absolute wonder and unquenchable curiosity? I don't see it that way.

From my limited point of view, it appears that this pressure is exerted to generate scores that will draw major corporations and their investments into communities and to elect or reelect public officials and to make even greater profits for the companies who produce the materials and assessments associated with increasing achievement-test scores. To do this on the backs of small children through undue pressures exerted upon their teachers is, to me, nothing short of immoral.

Let's remind ourselves of the reasons we entered this profession. We came to lead children into life, to lead them to live with honesty and dignity and integrity. We came to help them gain the tools needed to question, to think, to locate resources and search out multiple points of view as they work toward understandings. We came to help them realize that knowledge brings options and options bring choices and choices bring freedoms and with freedoms come responsibilities. We came not just to make them smarter or to fill their heads with facts and tidbits of information. Rather, we came to help them learn to live in a world that is filled with human beings who are much more alike than different if we look at them from the inside out rather than from the outside in. We came to help them learn to navigate the rest of *their* lives, not just to live through one year of our lives.

> **"True ease in writing comes from art, not chance,**
>
> **As those move easiest who have learned to dance.**
>
> **'Tis not enough no harshness gives offense.**
>
> **The sound must seem an echo to the sense."**
>
> —Alexander Pope

Remember that this work, the work of reading and writing, the work of studying craft, is only one small part of the greater vision in your work as a teacher. In all your work with children, let nothing you do and no words you say take from a child his or her dignity as a human being, compromise his or her integrity as a learner, or strip his or her identity as a reader or writer or mathematician or scientist or dancer or athlete or artist or...

It is really this simple: build your professional knowledge base and use your common sense. And above all else—keep your focus on the children.

Appendix

Anchor Texts to Support Audible and Visual Craft Study

Audible Craft Study

1. Repeated Words

Click, Clack, Moo:
Cows That Type
Written by Doreen Cronin
Illustrated by Betsy Lewin
Simon & Schuster, 2000.
ISBN 0-689-83213-3

2. Repetition of a Specific Phrase

The Other Side
Written by Jacqueline Woodson
Illustrated by E. B. Lewis
G.P. Putnam's Sons, 2001.
ISBN 0-399-23116-1

In November
Written by Cynthia Rylant
Illustrated by Jill Kastner
Harcourt, 2000.
ISBN 0-15-201076-9

Whoever You Are
Written by Mem Fox
Illustrated by Leslie Staub
Harcourt, 1997.
ISBN 0-15-200787-3

The Sunsets of Miss Olivia Wiggins
Written by Lester L. Laminack
Illustrated by Constance R. Bergum
Peachtree, 1998.
ISBN 1-56145-139-8

The Magic Hat
Written by Mem Fox
Illustrated by Tricia Tusa
Harcourt, 2002.
ISBN 0-15-201025-4

3. Proper Names (street names, names of neighbors, etc.)

Come On, Rain!
Written by Karen Hesse
Illustrated by Jon J. Muth
Scholastic, 1999.
ISBN 0-590-33125-6

Uptown
Written and illustrated
by Brian Collier
Henry Holt, 2000.
ISBN 0-8050-5721-8

4. Brand Names

Uptown
Written and illustrated
by Brian Collier
Henry Holt, 2000.
ISBN 0-8050-5721-8

5. Honoring Speech

The Other Side
Written by Jacqueline Woodson
Illustrated by E. B. Lewis
G.P. Putnam's Sons, 2001.
ISBN 0-399-23116-1

Amber on the Mountain
Written by Tony Johnston
Illustrated by Robert Duncan
Dial, 1994.
ISBN 0-8037-1219-7

6. Sound Effects (onomatopoeia)

Roller Coaster
Written and illustrated
by Marla Frazee
Harcourt, 2003.
ISBN 0-15-204554-6

Mr. George Baker
Written by Amy Hest
Illustrated by Jon J. Muth
Candlewick Press, 2004.
ISBN 0-7636-1233-2

Achoo! Bang! Crash!
The Noisy Alphabet
Written and illustrated
by Ross MacDonald
Roaring Brook Press, 2003.
ISBN 0-7613-1796-1

7. Figurative Language (metaphors, similes, personification)

Scarecrow
Written by Cynthia Rylant
Illustrated by Lauren Stringer
Harcourt, 1998.
ISBN 0-15-201084-X

In November
Written by Cynthia Rylant
Illustrated by Jill Kastner
Harcourt, 2000.
ISBN 0-15-201076-9

The Barn Owls
Written by Tony Johnston
Illustrated by Deborah Kogan Ray
Talewinds (Charlesbridge), 2000.
ISBN 0-88106-981-7

Visual Craft Study

1. Italics

The Sunsets of Miss Olivia Wiggins
Written by Lester L. Laminack
Illustrated by Constance R. Bergum
Peachtree, 1998.
ISBN 1-56145-139-8

The Horned Toad Prince
Written by Jackie Mims Hopkins
Illustrated by Michael Austin
Peachtree, 2000.
ISBN 1- 56145-195-9

Jake's 100th Day of School
Written by Lester L. Laminack
Illustrated by Judy Love
Peachtree, 2006.
ISBN 1-56145-355-2

2. Stretching Out the Print

"Hurty Feelings"
Written by Helen Lester
Illustrated by Lynn Munsinger
Houghton Mifflin, 2004.
ISBN 13: 978-0-618-41082-8

Roller Coaster
Written and illustrated
by Marla Frazee
Harcourt, 2003.
ISBN 0-15-204554-6

The Recess Queen
Written by Alexis O'Neill
Illustrated by Laura Huliska-Beith
Scholastic, 2002.
ISBN 0-439-20637-5

3. Stacking Words

Uptown
Written and illustrated
by Brian Collier
Henry Holt, 2000.
ISBN 0-8050-5721-8

Come On, Rain!
Written by Karen Hesse
Illustrated by Jon J. Muth
Scholastic, 1999.
ISBN 0-590-33125-6

Jake's 100th Day of School
Written by Lester L. Laminack
Illustrated by Judy Love
Peachtree, 2006.
ISBN 1-56145-355-2

The Recess Queen
Written by Alexis O'Neill
Illustrated by Laura Huliska-Beith
Scholastic, 2002.
ISBN 0-439-20637-5

4. Sentence Fragments

The Recess Queen
Written by Alexis O'Neill
Illustrated by Laura Huliska-Beith
Scholastic, 2002.
ISBN 0-439-20637-5

Mr. George Baker
Written by Amy Hest
Illustrated by Jon J. Muth
Candlewick Press, 2004.
ISBN 0-7636-1233-2

Jake's 100th Day of School
Written by Lester L. Laminack
Illustrated by Judy Love
Peachtree, 2006.
ISBN 1-56145-355-2

Scarecrow
Written by Cynthia Rylant
Illustrated by Lauren Stringer
Harcourt, 1998.
ISBN 0-15-201084-X

5. Parentheses

Dog Eared
Written and illustrated
by Amanda Harvey
Doubleday, 2002.
ISBN 0-385-72911-1

6. Dashes to Add an Afterthought

What You Know First
Written by Patricia MacLachlan
Illustrated by Barry Moser
Joanna Cotler Books
(HarperCollins), 1995.
ISBN 0-06-024413-5

Mr. George Baker
Written by Amy Hest
Illustrated by Jon J. Muth
Candlewick Press, 2004.
ISBN 0-7636-1233-2

In November
Written by Cynthia Rylant
Illustrated by Jill Kastner
Harcourt, 2000.
ISBN 0-15-201076-9

7. Extra Line Spaces

My Lucky Day
Written and illustrated
by Keiko Kasza
G. P. Putnam's Sons, 2003.
ISBN 0-399-23874-3

References

Professional Resources

Fox, M. (1993). *Radical reflections*. San Diego, CA: Harcourt.

LeGuin, U. K. (1998). *Steering the craft*. Portland, Oregon: Eighth Mountain Press.

Lyon, G. E. (1999). *Where I'm from: Where poems come from*. Spring, TX: Absey & Company.

Murray, D. (1989). *Expecting the unexpected*. Portsmouth, NH: Heinemann.

Murray, D. (1996). *Crafting a life*. Portsmouth, NH: Heinemann.

Ray, K. W. (1999). *Wondrous words*. Urbana, IL: NCTE.

Sloane, W. (1979). *The craft of writing*. New York: W. W. Norton and Company.

Zinsser, W. (2001). *On writing well*. New York: Harper.

Web Links

www.lesterlaminack.com
My website will give you and your students another way to know me as a writer. You will discover a bit about my life and answers to a few of the questions children often ask during my school visits. You will also be able to keep abreast of my publishing and consulting schedule. So log on and let me know what you think.

www.soentpiet.com
Chris Soentpiet's talent as an illustrator is extraordinary and is only glimpsed in *Saturdays and Teacakes*. Take a look at his website and explore the depth of his talent. You'll find ways to order his other books, prints of his art, and how to book him to visit your school.

www.peachtree-online.com
Visit the website of the publisher of my picture books for children, Peachtree Publishers. You'll find many wonderful authors, illustrators, and titles here as well. So go ahead, browse a bit.